AF270098

CISTERCIAN FATHERS SERIES : NUMBER FORTY-FIVE

JOHN OF FORD

SERMONS ON THE SONG OF SONGS, V

JOHN of FORD

Volume Five
(SERMONS 62-82)

Translated by
WENDY MARY BECKETT

CISTERCIAN FATHERS SERIES : NUMBER FORTY-FIVE

SERMONS ON THE FINAL VERSES OF THE SONG OF SONGS

CISTERCIAN PUBLICATIONS: *Kalamazoo, Michigan 1983*

*The editors wish to express their appreciation to Mr John Nixon
for his help in preparing the manuscript for publication*

This translation is based on the critical Latin edition of the sermons prepared by Edmund Mikkers and Hilary Costello and published in the series CORPUS CHRISTIANORUM, *Continuatio Mediaevalis* XVII & XVIII.

Latin title: *Ioannis de Forda, Super extremam partem cantici canticorum sermones cxx.*

Available in Great Britain and Europe through

A. R. Mowbray & Co. Ltd St Thomas House
Becket Street, Oxford OX1 1SJ

Library of Congress Cataloguing in Publication Data (Revised)

John, Abbot of Ford.
    Sermons on the final verses of the Song of Songs.

    (Cistercian Fathers series ; no. 29, 39, 43, 44, 45)
    Translation of Ioannis de Forda Super extremam
partem Cantici canticorum sermones CXX.
    On Spine: on the Song of Songs.
    Includes bibliographical references.
    CONTENTS: 1. Sermons 1-14.—2. Sermons 15-28.—
3. Sermons 29-46.—4. Sermons 47-61.—5. Sermons 62-82.
    1. Bible. O.T. Song of Solomon—Sermons.
2. Catholic Church—Sermons. 3. Sermons,
English—Translations from Latin. 4. Sermons,
Latin—Translations into English. I. Title.
II. Title: On the Song of Songs.
BS1485.J6413   223'.907   77-3697
ISBN 0-87907-629-1 (v. 1)   AAACR1
ISBN 0-87907-644-5 (v. 4)

Book design by Gale Akins.
Printed in the United States of America.

TABLE OF CONTENTS

SERMONS

Sermon Sixty-Two	1
Sermon Sixty-Three	14
Sermon Sixty-Four	24
Sermon Sixty-Five	36
Sermon Sixty-Six	50
Sermon Sixty-Seven	62
Sermon Sixty-Eight	76
Sermon Sixty-Nine	86
Sermon Seventy	96
Sermon Seventy-One	107
Sermon Seventy-Two	118
Sermon Seventy-Three	130
Sermon Seventy-Four	144
Sermon Seventy-Five	155
Sermon Seventy-Six	168
Sermon Seventy-Seven	184
Sermon Seventy-Eight	197
Sermon Seventy-Nine	209
Sermon Eighty	219
Sermon Eighty-One	231
Sermon Eighty-Two	242

SERMON SIXTY-TWO

The beginning of the sixty-second sermon.
Of the manifold return of the synagogue
to belief in Christ, and how universal joy is felt
at her returning, and how great will be the
result of this change of heart.

'RETURN, RETURN, O SHULAMITE;
return, return, that we may gaze on
you. Why should you look upon the
Shulamite as upon a dance before two
armies?'*

At first sight, these words strike a chord in
the memory and demand our attention. They
bring to mind the ancient story of Abishag,
the Shulamite, who was sought 'throughout
all the land of Israel',* when they were looking for a very beautiful girl who would keep
David warm.* He was then in his old age,
very cold, and unable to find warmth in the
clothes that covered him. So they brought
this maiden to him, to stay at his side and
keep him warm, and at night to sleep in his
arms to keep him warm.* 'But', as we are told
in scripture, 'the king did not have intercourse with her.'* So we have a historical
record that, though she embraced the king
tenderly and warmed him with the most
flattering intimacy, this young woman remained a virgin. Surely, those who were

Sg 6:12

1 K 1:3

1 K 1:2

1 K 1:3

1 K 1:4

privy to so great a secret could well be roused to profound wonder at the integrity of such virginity? When she came forth from the royal bed chamber, they might well advance to greet her, looking upon her with hero-worship and exclaiming: 'Return, return, O Shulamite; return, return, that we may gaze on you.'*

2. But these are words from the distant past, and long ago their shadow passed away. The truth, though, that was faintly outlined beneath their veil, endures to this day, or rather, 'it will endure to eternity',* waiting for there to be a fulfillment of what is still held concealed within it, as if under a seal.* Moreover, the chilly old age of King David which could not be warmed by clothing, is an unmistakeable portent of the state of the christian faith at the end of time. Christ, the true David, speaks openly of the coldness of those times, when he declares: 'Because wickedness is multiplied, most men's love will grow cold.'*

This is why, in regard to the coldness of this 'old age', as if providing from afar for himself and the feeble members of his church, Christ cries, very lovingly and providently, to the Father, 'Even to old age and gray hairs, O God, forsake me not.'* It was about this old age, too, that Solomon was preaching, using several different figures of speech, when he said, 'The almond tree will blossom, the locust will be heavy with food, the caper bush will be scattered abroad.'* He goes on to other images also, all very deliberately and plainly expressing the weariness of this extreme and feeble age.

Now it follows that, in his old age, David will have no lack at all of ample clothing, because scripture says: 'This generation' of believers 'will not pass away until all these things come to pass.'* Equally, no want of wisdom or knowledge will press upon him, because, as Daniel says, 'Many will pass away, and knowledge will increase.'* No, it is from 'the multiplication of wickedness'* that, quite certainly, this senile cold will draw its power, until none of the 'garments' we have been speaking of, will be able to bring it warmth.

3. But when those days come, there will still be some who are faithful to our Lord, our 'King David', and who are still animated by some little spark of charity, despite so great a coldness. Surely they will be forced, by a healthy necessity, to follow David's course with regard to their safety and life? And no other recourse will be found except to seek out for him the most beautiful maiden in the whole land of Israel, so that she 'may wait upon the king and be his nurse; that she may sleep in his arms and warm our lord the king'.* What maiden is this? It is the people of Israel, whose first husband, God, will take thought to himself, remembering His youth, as Jeremiah says: 'I remembered you, pitying your youth'?* Again, we find scripture referring to her, when it says: 'As were the days of your youth, so will be the days of your old age.'* For by the extraordinary mercy of God, this virgin will be as young as ever in the days of her old age! She will be 'a spectacle to men and angels;'* her

Mt 24:34

Dn 12:4
Cf. Mt 24:12

1 K 1:2

Jr 2:2

Dt 33:25

1 Co 4:9

limbs are aged, yet they will appear most beautiful and desirable to the husband of her girlhood.*

4. What precisely does it mean, this praise, this loud cry? What 'glory' is it 'to God on high',* what joy 'on earth, to men who are God's friends,'* who stand on either side, rejoicing in one great exclamation: 'Return, return, O Shulamite: return, return, that we may gaze on you'?* Poor little maid, the wind of God's anger blew on her in the past, and she was scattered over the whole country-side, but, as it says in scripture: 'He who scattered Israel will gather him.'* 'The north will be told: give up; and the south: do not withhold.'* The east, as well, and the west, will be warned to make no delay in returning those whom they have taken captive.* So, coming back from the four corners of the earth, Israel will find the church of the gentiles waiting at all four corners, so that the ark of the Lord may be borne into Jerusalem amid the music of drum and fife and many holocausts of praise.* And then our maiden Israel will hear from all sides the reverent voices of those who delight to see her; they will say, 'Return, return, O Shulamite, return, return, that we may gaze on you.'*

Indeed, it is something worth 'gazing upon', something very well worth deep contemplation, the way dry bones have freshly come to life, and, as in the prophecy of Ezekiel, a huge and powerful army stands where but recently there was a heap of dry bones.* Obviously, to have seen Lazarus come forth from the tomb would have been a sublime

spectacle,* and no less great would have been   *Cf. Jn 11:44*
the sight of the three young men, but one in
perseverance, who emerged from the fire of
the Babylonian furnace completely unharmed
and untouched.* Yet can these, or sights   *Cf. Dn 3:92*
like them, compare to that marvelous sight
reserved for the end of time, when the virgin
Israel* will remember the days of her youth   *Cf. Jr 31:21*
and feel ashamed of her scandalous and longlasting widowhood?* She will beat her breast   *Cf. Is 54:4*
and her thigh and begin to return to her first
husband.*   *Cf. Hos 2:7*

5. She will return from the lands of the
rising sun, believing and proclaiming the holy
Incarnation of the Word of God. She will
return from the lands of the setting sun, proclaiming and praising the Passion, gladly
suffered by Christ Jesus for the salvation of
the world. She will return, too, from the
north, praising and honoring his power, when
he rose in glory to triumph over death and the
author of death.* And lastly, she will return   *Cf. Ac 3:15*
from the south lands, beholding the majesty
of the King of heaven, who arranges all things
in heaven and on earth, according to his
will.*   *Cf. Ps 114*

6. Or, if you prefer: because it was to the
very ends of the earth that the sons of Israel,
as we know, were expelled by God's decree
on account of their sins, these far-off lands
seem to symbolize something perverse and
very distant from the holy city of Jerusalem.
So the virgin Israel was sent out into the east
when she departed from the love of her spouse
and shamefully renewed the ignoble state in
which she was born, just as the prophet said:

Is 63:19

'We have become as in the beginning, when you did not rule over us, when we did not call ourselves by the name of the Lord.'* She was thrust out, also, towards the west, when for them, the Sun of true wisdom set, so that all the mystery of the law and the lighted lamp of prophecy was completely lost to their sight. Then she was driven away to the north, for she was exposed to the shame of captivity and the jeers and mockeries of all nations, and in so great a calamity she did not open her ear nor see 'the rod of waiting'.*

Jr 1:11

Finally, she was cast away to the lands of the south, because she thinks that she is living as if in the full light of noon, and it is in darkness of the densest gloom. With eyes that are blind, and yet somehow open, although the Sun of justice is already lighting up all the earth with noontide brightness, she still continues to blunder insanely forward, raging against him with her old hatred, as if she were a boiling pot.

So to the east she is without grace, abandoned to what she is by birth. To the west, she is deprived of the light of knowledge, completely misunderstanding what she reads in her scriptures. To the north, she is abandoned to war, hunger, captivity and disgrace, and throughout it all, she keeps her

Cf. Ex 32:9

neck rigid and unbowed.* To the hot south, she is a persecutor of the Lamb of God, with ever fresh and incurable fury, never cooling in her hate, as if under the hot sun of noon. How far away from God's justice are these lands, how far removed from christian love and tenderness! But what is far away from justice, is close at hand to love and tenderness, and what is at a great distance with regard to merit, abounding grace considers very near indeed. For, as the apostle points out, 'where sin abounded, grace did more abound.'*   *Rm 5:20*

7. To go on, then, with this image of the Shulamite, Abishag will return—and the name, 'Abishag', means 'crying aloud'. Abishag will return, crying aloud in the distress of her heart;* yes, she will return to herself, return   *Cf. Ps 38:7* to the days of her youth,* return to her Lord,   *Cf. Jl 1:8* Christ, King David, return to the love of the church. She will return to herself through the loud lamentations of repentance; she will return to her early youth by renewing her first fervor; she will return to King David by a new bethrothal of immense charity; she will return to the peace of the church through being united in her holy company. Then, once more, she will stand before the Lord, King David and give him warmth, 'she will sleep in his arms and warm him.'*   *1 K 1:2*

I say, 'she will stand', because the virgin Israel has fallen down. She herself can do nothing to help herself rise, but there is One who will raise her.* It is He who says, 'Virgin   *Cf. Ps 41:8* Israel, return to your own cities.'* Yes, it is   *Jr 31:21* He who is both able and willing to restore to her the glory of the virginity, lost after so many and such grievous wrongs. As He says in words of compassionate love: 'At least now, call me: 'My father, you are the guide of my virginity.'* So Abishag will stand before King   *Jr 3:4* David, fixing her eyes upon him, and in her turn, letting him look upon her. She will gaze upon him, and this will make her form resemble his; she will offer herself for him to look on her, so that she may lay her whole conscience completely before him. She will stand in his presence, in order that, whether he sits or walks or takes his meals, she may 'warm' him. Of course, to warm him while he sleeps, she herself must lie down beside him, and sleep in his arms.

8. Abishag will stand, therefore, and when Christ her king is working, she will work with him. In other words, when he is seated in his teacher's chair, she will sit with him, to teach and instruct many nations. When he is walking also, she will run to and fro, 'from one nation to another, from one kingdom to another people,'* helping in the task of preaching. By building up these peoples, she will rejoice the heart of King David, as if with a glorious banquet of the best wine. Yet, the most delicate and personal joy is reserved for the marriage bed, one that does not diminish her virginal modesty, but deepens and sanctifies it. Abishag sleeps on David's breast, and he too sleeps on Abishag's breast, and the most intimate 'breast' of holy contemplation makes each a source of warmth for the other. The joy of the bride rejoicing in her spouse is the same joy that the spouse feels, rejoicing in his bride. So they grow warm, by mutually embracing each other, and these memories of past delights make David grow warm once more in his old age, since, through Israel, the christian faith will regain the strength of its former beauty, and love, grown cold, will regain its fervor.

*Ps 105:13

9. So then, when the church of the gentiles has 'gone down to the orchard of nuts, to look at the fruits of the valley and see whether the vines had budded and the pomegranates were in flower,'* and when she fails to find in her orchard what she was seeking, and came away from it sorrowful, she mourned, and said that she 'knew nothing, and that she was disturbed by the chariots of Aminadab',* meaning by this the terrible judgements of God. After all this, seeing that her orchard had told her nothing to make her happy, she had every reason to long for the approach of this Shulamite, every reason to break out into this great cry, and exclaimed: 'Return, O Shulamite, return, return, that we may gaze on you!'*

10. Indeed, your return is already all too necessary, for here on earth everything has already become lifeless and chill. Already the abyss of our sluggish tepidity calls out to the abyss of God's loving tenderness,* the only direction from which we can be renewed. It calls out 'in the sound of God's cataracts, that is, in the sound of the apostles and prophets, who faithfully promise us that you will return. May it come, 'O captive daughter of Zion',* the solemn day we are awaiting, the day of your salvation! How long will you go on grieving, turned away and defrauded of your own rightful heritage? After a widowhood has already lasted so long, remember the covenant made in ancient days! Lift up your heart and long for the sign of reconciliation, saying to God, 'Let him kiss me with the kiss of his mouth.'* You can quite

certainly come back to your beloved; you can quite certainly find healing for your wounds and a renewal of your covenant. However desperate your bruises, you have a sure remedy; in the treasury of the king, there is laid up for you for all eternity, your redemption.

Sg 6:12

'Return,' then, 'return, O Shulamite,'* Zion your mother, awaits you, the church of the patriarchs and prophets, the whole assembly of your forefathers. The blessed company of the heavenly spirits awaits you, for it is through you and from your ranks that their glorious city will one day be completed. Last of all, your most beloved spouse, remembering no more your past unfriendliness, opens wide to embrace you the arms which he stretched out on the cross.* And as for us, the last to be cut off from the wild olive tree and grafted, through no merit of our own, onto your stock,* given a share, solely through grace, in your richness,* because of the skill of our holy Grafter, we long for your return, not only without envy, but with most benevolent charity.

Cf. Bernard, SC 68:4; SBOp 2:199; CF 40:21.

Cf. Rm 11:24

Cf. Rm 11:17

Sg 6:12

11. So, 'return, return, O Shulamite!'* To see that face of yours, transparently bright, recreated in all the beauty of its youth after all the wrinkles of old age have been smoothed over, this will indeed be something for us to look upon, and it will be a looking-glass, as well! We shall look upon her and draw a lesson. Now that the fire of love is certainly growing old, we too begin to age, and, as holy Job commented, our wrinkles bear witness against us.* 'Return,' then,

Cf. Jb 16:9

'O Shulamite,'* so that in gazing upon your   *Sg 6:12*
face we may find strength to wonder at it and
to imitate it. From the light of your face, or
so we believe, a new serenity will arise, and
beholding the glory of your countenance, we
shall be transformed into the same image.*   *Cf. 2 Co 5:18*

For all these reasons, and for each single
one of them: 'Return, return, return!' Oh yes,
'Return, that we may gaze on you!'* Indeed,   *Sg 6:12*
it is not possible to frustrate God's expectations, powerful as he is to answer our
prayers with the richest blessings.

12. Then, very aptly, the verse continues:
'Why should you look upon the Shulamite as
upon a dance before two armies?'* It is not   *Sg 7:1*
quite clear whether it is the spouse or his companions who is speaking, but what is perfectly
clear, is that it is the Holy Spirit who is speaking. Moreover, it bears this mark of the
spouse, that from whom the spirit received it.
Indeed, what is said is of very great terse-
ness, yet a compliment of the highest value.
It would be impossible to praise the Shulamite more concisely but more fully.

'Why do you look upon the Shulamite', it
says, 'as upon a dance between two armies?'*   *Ibid.*
Dances are for those who sing, armies are for
those who fight. So the sons of Israel are
marching out singing, to fight the Lord's
battles with a high heart. In consequence, the
careful conducting of warfare does not stand
in the way of a song of praise, and neither
does overflowing joy enfeeble the hands of
the brave with its false security. No, 'there is
the high praise of God upon their lips,'* as in   *Ps 149:6*
those who enjoy themselves and lead the

dance, 'and a two-edged sword in their hand',* as with those who are going out to fight,' to bring down vengeance on the nations, and punishment on all the peoples.'* Then, since 'evening is coming, they suffer hunger like dogs,' and this makes them 'go around the city.'* In other words, they will traverse the whole world in their preaching, so that they may compensate for what they once lost from their own salvation by saving many others. After so long a period of fast, the only meal that can satisfy their intense hunger is that of saving the whole world. For, as scripture tells us, 'the destruction that is decreed will overflow with righteousness,'* and righteousness, making the last age of all pleasing to God, will redress the balance of all the ages that they have lost.

'Why should you look', O church of the gentiles, bride of the Lord Jesus, when that day comes, 'why should you look upon the Shulamite as on a dance between two armies?'* This Shulamite will know both the utter joy of victory and the utter victory of salvation. There will be in her hand 'a two-edged sword,'* not as in the days gone by, when religious faith was seen as permitting great slaughter among nations, but with great life for souls springing from the sword's edge, and the only blood, that of penitence, the only death, that of sin. Those swords will win back for themselves the ideal of perfection the apostles taught, which is their rightful heritage. They will rejoice indeed, that they too are sending sickles in their fields, as once they rejoiced in their harvest.* Those who

Ibid.

Ps 149:7

Ps 59:6

Is 10:22

Sg 7:1

Ps 149:6

Cf. Is 9:3

once exulted to divide their spoils,* carefully
and happily, will also exult in the shouts of
their triumphant conquerors, and the exulta-
tion will be fully as great on both sides.
Receiving for their portion, the very rich
fruit of their labor, they have brought grace
and peace to the peoples of the earth, and
offered glory and praise to God, the Giver
of all things, who, with his only Son and
the Holy Spirit, lives and reigns,
for ever and ever,
Amen.

The beginning of the sixty-third sermon. How this verse is very meaningful for the soul that loves God; and whether it is by angels or by the maidens that the bride of the Word is warned to turn from the sorrow which she said distressed her, and return to her former tranquility; and how lovingly the spouse sets about praising her afresh.

'RETURN, RETURN, O SHULAMITE; return, return, that we may gaze on you. Why should you look upon the Shulamite as upon a dance between two armies?'*

Sg 6:12

I realize that you are waiting for a second course to be served from these words, so as to build up your charity. I am ready to meet your expectation as far as is in me, but you must not withhold your part of it, to prevail upon the Father of spirits that the devotional effect may be up to standard. And to have a clearer understanding of the sequence of these words, let us look at what has preceded them and link the two together.

2. The bride of the Word (and this means, the holy soul) clings to God with all her heart, with the utmost earnestness and a single-minded intensity. She is deeply perturbed and very humiliated by the great compliments

14

paid her by the daughters of Zion which, as she sees it, make her too important. As was said before, then, she 'goes down' into the 'orchard' of her conscience,* to take a long, *Sg 6:11* searching look at everything that is in it that the daughters of Zion have so splendidly singled out for attention. Moreover, the bride does not take with her into this task of investigation, her own personal self-love, knowing too well that it is seized early by others and its judgements are blind. So, having carefully examined the buds of her nuts, fruits, vines and pomegranates, that is, her holiness, her humility, and the charity she has for God and her brothers, she comes forward to give her honest assessment of their fruits of love. As the verse before this one makes quite clear, she has found every one of them below what she would have wanted, and the valuation of the daughters of Zion is too flattering.

3. As a modest woman, is it not natural that she should blush? As one who fears God, is it not natural that she is deeply afraid? Under the double weight of shame and fear, she dispells or at least forestalls the weight of itching vanity, and can say: 'I knew nothing; my soul disturbed me, on account of the chariots of Aminadab.'* When she says, 'I *Ibid.* knew nothing', she is relinquishing all right to make her own judgements on her personal conscience. Clearly, she agrees with the apostle in claiming: 'Neither do I judge myself, but there is one who judges me, and that is the Lord.'* Then by 'the chariots of Amminadab', *1 Co 4:3,4* as was discussed above at greater length, she indicates that she has every reason to feel

greatly afraid of God's terrible and searching judgements. He alone knows the secrets of the hearts of men, and can assess their desires and motives.*

What can be done now, when the Lord's bride is so intensely alarmed? Only that the friends of the spouse, namely, the holy angels and the spirits of the blest, who keep him company, should not delay to encourage her with their loving comfort. Think, then, of those heavens, utterly serene, bending humbly down to the bride, an effect of the very great love of her spouse. Think of them pleading graciously at her side, coaxing her with their gentle entreaties and saying, 'Return, return, O Shulamite; return, return, that we may gaze on you.'*

4. Return, return, from those uncontrolled excesses, which disturb your soul, on account of the chariots of Amminadab.* The four aspects of those chariot wheels disturb you, naturally enough. You are worried by the keenness of their judgements; you are worried by their inflexible justice; you are worried by the force of their rushing movement; you are worried by their absolute standard of impartiality. But when you look at all these aspects at once, they do more than worry you, they 'disturb' you. So you have a disturbance made up of four elements. All the same, leave it now. 'Return, return, O Shulamite; return, return'* to the serenity of your former peace and happiness. Beware, bride of the Lord, because immoderate excesses of overflowing joy are as dangerous as those of overwhelming fear. Steer a prudent course; let neither

storm sink you, nor abyss engulf you. If you yield to one side more than is right, you are very near to being swallowed up by the other.

Remember also, that you are being borne along by the Spirit of divine love, whirled away to the sacred bridal chamber of your spouse in heaven by 'a chariot of fire and fiery horses.'* Come then, O Shulamite, set about controlling the bit and spurs of your horses with the scarlet charity of your heavenly spouse. There must be no risk of their galloping headlong through too much fervor, or of their dawdling along through over-timidity. Fear must not outrun hope, but neither must hope get the start on fear. And zeal for justice and hatred of injustice must obey the command of God's Spirit, kept to an even and controlled pace by the charioteer in control.

Return, then, return, O Shulamite, from pondering upon your deformity and imperfection. Return, I say, return to considering also your graciousness and beauty. Try, at least, to regard the causes of your self-dissatisfaction in such a way that you can also recognize that there are some things that give satisfaction to your spouse. Do not ignore that you are black, but at the same time, do not be unaware that you are beautiful.* Of course, it is a great thing, and very praiseworthy, to be unaffected by the well-meaning compliments, however great, not of foolish women, but of the daughters of Zion! But, in the same way, it also demands virtue to restrain the excesses of fear and to say boldly to your soul when it 'disturbs' you: 'Why are you cast down,

Cf. 2 K 2:11

Cf. Sg 1:4

Ps 42:5

Ps 116:7

1 K 1:2

my soul, and why do you disturb me?'* If you are disturbed in my own regard, O my soul, at any rate rise up and take comfort from your God, my spouse. Certainly I do not rest in you, nor you in me, but this is neither possible nor necessary. Yet, 'turn back, my soul, to your rest,'* your sure rest, your changeless and joyous God, your Lord who has given now good things, good things that never cease.

5. Lay aside, therefore, this pallor, which sudden grief has brought into your face, and this veil of shame which we see enshrouding you. Take them both from your face and let your countenance once more be animated by its former charm. This will give us the joy of seeing you joyful. How much longer is that countenance, richly blessed with beauty, to be lined with wrinkles and covered with the stains of neglect? At all events, look at us, and then we, in our turn, will delight to gaze upon what, here below, is the holiness, peace, joy, and eternity of our city, and gaze upon us, your fellow citizens, who live here. So that we, in turn, may gaze on you, our fellow citizen; for the sight will transform you and make you very lovely, of its own accord, and we shall gaze upon you then with even greater pleasure. For you are the fairest in all the land of Israel, you deserve all honor, you who stand before King David and sleep in his arms and warm him and keep him from the cold.*

Christ is our David, and here among his angels, everything that is in him or within his orbit, takes warmth from him. From his face, too, there issues an impetuous stream of fire,* inflaming all heaven with its charity, ravishing it with its goodness, intoxicating it with delight. Yet, on this frozen earth of yours, the head of Jesus 'is wet with dew, and his locks with the drops of night.'* Down on earth he is a poor man, down on earth he is cold. He is weak there, he hungers and thirsts, he can scarcely find 'a place to lay his head.'* There his greatness is harassed by manifold injuries, and he struggles with his whole body. As long as he sees that his bride is distressed, he endures not to be taken down from his cross. Your duty, then, O bride of the Lord, is to stay beside him in his suffering, to give him warmth in his weakness, with pure heart and body to soothe his many needs with whatever remedy you can find.

Cf. Dn 7:10

Sg 5:2

Mt 8:20

If the words of the spouse's companions, namely, the spirits of the blessed, are to raise the heart of the trembling bride to happier thoughts, and to encourage her to rise up to greater joy and hope, then they will be words like these, or something similar, that they will speak into her ear.

6. But, on the other hand, it could be the maidens who are speaking, sharing in their mother's suffering with loving and daughterly affection. Then, obviously, when the bride says, 'My soul disturbed me,'* they immediately come to her support. They console her with their encouragement, with whatever consolation they can find. Return, they say, O fairest of women, from this great and deep disturbance of yours, which we see, and see

Cf. Sg 6:11

with sorrow, has suddenly ravaged your countenance. Return from the dismay this fear has caused; return from this painful sense of shame; return from this weary listlessness; return from the sadness and heaviness of your grief.

Think, what hope remains for your daughters, if 'the chariots of Amminadab' so disturb your soul? If the bride of our Lord feels such extreme dread before the tribunal of her spouse, what ground for confidence can we have, we who have never come anywhere near his bridal chamber? Put on an expression, now, that looks more peaceful, and however far we have gone in our indiscreet admiration of you, overlook it with motherly kindness. From now on, we shall try to be more prudent in this respect, and we shall take care to protect your integrity by keeping our praise within bounds.

7. And perhaps it is for this reason that the daughters of Zion do not, this time, address the bride as 'fairest of women',* or by any other high-sounding title, but prefer to call her 'Shulamite', with its implications of captivity. They diminish her by expressly using a humbler name for her, as if this were the direct result of their reconciliation. Clearly, they do not dare to praise her openly, but they give a silent hint of their admiration of her beauty by prudently using this mysterious name, which conceals a certain ambiguity. Under the cover of calling her 'a captive', therefore, yet using the image of the Shulamite who attended upon King David, they are saying that she is the loveliest

Cf. Sg 6:1

woman in all Israel, the only one worthy to sleep in the spouse's arms and stand always before him, seeing him and being seen by him, the one who warms him and keeps away the cold.*

Cf. 1 K 1:2

Although, for that matter, the very term 'captive' can be taken in two different ways. It can be seen as the captivity of misery, the unhappy slavery under which 'all creation groans and is in labor, even until now.'* Or it can be taken as the captivity of love, where the soul that loves God is led in chains of charity.

Rm 8:22

8. Of course, this is a most joyful and free 'captivity', the captivity in which Christ once 'ascended, and lead captivity captive.'* This was when he bore in triumph to his Father the proofs of his victorious combat, which were such splendid booty of captives, such blessed spoils of freedom, so many thousand rejoicing people. Now, it is with these captives that the Lord's bride is seen as having some intimate connection. Whenever she falls into ecstacy, she 'ascends with shouts of joy'* in company with her spouse, not through the efforts of her own virtue, but because she is a captive, led away in the hands of her spouse and the angels. Blindly, more passive than active, she is for the moment drawn violently away from herself, seized, carried away and made prisoner in some country completely strange to her. It is not a case only of captivity, but of 'captivity captive', where love alone is the victor, and the whole reason, memory and will of men surrenders in voluntary captivity to him who

Eph 4:8

Cf. Ps 47:5

seizes and carries away his captive.

9. The result is that the spouse is grateful to the daughters of Zion for giving the bride this new name, and uses it himself, though in order to praise her again, when he says: 'What will you see in the Shulamite except a dance between two armies?'* Then words are addressed to the group of maidens, just in case the bride's humble speech should have made them think anything less of her and they should have less regard than usual for their mother. He restores them, therefore, to their earlier admiration and emulous love for her by this short but wonderfully pregnant phrase: 'What will you see in the Shulamite except a dance between two armies?'*

The spouse appears to be reminding the daughters of Zion of the miracle that happened long ago at the fall of Jericho.* It crashed to the ground amid 'the singing of armies', namely, when the ark of the Lord was carried around it, amid the bray of the trumpets and the loud cries of the shouting children of Israel.* The spouse is implying that the bride has achieved something of the same nature within her, inasmuch as she has overthrown all worldly vanity in her heart. She has made a very careful circuit of her soul and hurled down from its foundations every loftiness of her own soul that could proudly rear itself up against the humble glory of her spouse.

10. The 'singing', then, is the humble love she feels for God alone, a love that keeps harmoniously united to him. This love, as is only right, gives to him alone the glory of

everything that he does in heaven and on earth. Likewise, 'the armies' are her strong, wise dispositions, especially those that are 'trained for war'.* These undertake nothing at all in their own strength but rely solely on God their salvation, in whom they act with confidence, fight with vigor and attack in force.* So, as can be deduced from the words he uses, the spouse seems to go to meet his bride with triumphal acclamation, as if she were fresh from a victory, and his manner of greeting is a new form of praise.

He does not begin his new praises with her head, as we would expect, but starts from her feet, as if praising her in reverse. He says, 'How beautiful are your feet in their sandals, O prince's daughter!'* But these words deserve to have care and attention of their own, as they will, but only if by our prayers, we gain the presence of the spouse of the church, our Lord, Jesus Christ, who with God the
Father and the Holy Spirit,
lives and reigns, God,
for ever and ever.
Amen.

SERMON SIXTY-FOUR

The beginning of the sixty-fourth sermon.
How these words may be applied to the church of the gentiles, when she suffers with the daughter of Zion, that is, the synagogue, on account of her lengthy captivity; and why she calls on her, four times, to return. Why it is from her sandaled feet, rather than from her head, that the spouse begins to praise the returning synagogue.

'HOW BEAUTIFUL ARE YOUR FEET in their sandals, O prince's daughter!'* To link together in a natural sequence what goes before and after these words, it is necessary first to refer to what was said above. For there is not the slightest doubt that the voice we hear speaking here is the voice of the spouse, and a very loving voice, too, full of admiration. Moreover, the whole tune of this Song has as its principal and primary theme the most blissful and holy charity which joins and unites the church, in the Holy Spirit, to her heavenly spouse. So the first thing to be seen is how these words are to be applied to this bride. But the second is that, by God's grace, that other bride is not to be defrauded of her praise, for she has been uniquely endowed with the gift of love, and dares to call the Lord of glory, her spouse.

2. To recall for a minute, the context: The bride of God, who is the church, had gone down into her orchard and made a wise, careful investigation of everything that was within it. Then that saying of Solomon came into her mind, 'He who increases knowledge, increases sorrow.'* Everything she saw, consi- *Cf. Qo 1:18* dered individually, worried her, and taken all together, they 'disturbed' her, so that she broke out into a cry of distress: 'I knew nothing, my soul disturbed me, on account of the chariots of Aminadab.'* However, 'the *Sg 6:11* Lord is close to the broken-hearted,'* and the *Ps 34:18* Spirit of her spouse prompted her to recall what she has heard and read, that 'there is a healer in Israel and balm in Gilead'.* Her *Cf. Jr 8:22* wound may be swelling with infection, may, in fact, be beyond hope, yet God has administered a remedy. When God brings back to himself his former wife, to whom in the past, a bill of divorce was given, it pleases him, in these last days, to bring back afresh to her original form the bride who was gathered from the gentile nations. Already she is half-dead with cold, and he calls her back from her torpor to her first fervor.

3. So it is with tears in her voice that the gentile church calls out with eager entreaty to the daughter of Zion, still a captive, and addresses her as 'Shulamite'. Again and again she reiterates: 'Return, return,'* showing the *Sg 6:12* loving goodwill of her petition, as well as implying the very unhappy motive for her urgency and showing what an abundance of fruit she expects from her confidence. But

Cf. 1 Co 13:5

since charity must not be mercenary or 'seek what is her own',* by the frequent repetition of this word, she guarantees the sincerity and depth of the feelings of tenderness, affecting her with regard to the present enslavement of the synagogue, and of charity, for she longs to see her restored to the embraces of her first spouse.

It is clear that the heart of the spouse is moved by this, for, after his bride's entreaties and counsels, he again turns his eyes to this same Shulamite. In rich and accomplished terms of praise, he recounts what she will be like when she has begun to return, or rather, what she is already like, in his eyes. He has no fear how these unbounded praises may affect the bride to whom he is presently bound, lest perhaps they defile her with the scourge of envy, because now he sees how she counts on the Shulamite's return, and how she longs for her to be saved. On the contrary, when perhaps Israel is still far off, the bride is already hastening forward, lovingly and thoughtfully, to awaken in her an eagerness for the virtues that will be hers, after so long a time. Yet the eagerness is as much based on imitating her virtues as she is practised in being eager for them.

4. But what, I wonder, is the point of setting about this praise by starting at the feet, in fact, actually at the sandals? It seems to me that the spouse wanted to indicate to this bride who has come from the gentile nations, the reason for the divorce by which he is seen to have repudiated his former bride. The reason is clear enough; she was unaware

of grace, she did not seek for grace, and so she fell from grace. She had every wish to build for herself a house of justice, but the chosen cornerstone, the precious stone, she rashly rejected.* Therefore, she herself has been rejected, and the house which she built has been overthrown.   *Cf. Is 28:16*

Listen, too, to Isaiah: 'Because the daughters of Zion are haughty and walk with outstretched necks, glancing wantonly with their eyes, mincing along as they go, tinkling with their feet, the Lord will strike with a baldness the heads of the daughters of Zion.'* Alas,   *Is 3:16*
we see, and we groan over, the shameful and longlasting baldness of Zion's captive daughter. True Justice has appeared in fleshly lowliness, and with the very sharp razor of judgement, in a moment shaved away all the fine qualities with which, independent of grace, she thought herself adorned. It is obviously the folly of this self-conceit that preceded the baldness, as if deserving and causing it, and this is what the prophet is telling us when he says: 'Because the daughters of Zion are haughty.' 'Because' of this haughtiness, they do not proclaim and adore the glory of justifying grace, 'and they walk with outstretched necks', not seeking the help of grace and not giving thanks for helping grace. 'And they glance wantonly with their eyes', delighting with wanton folly in their own virtue, wherever they seem to be acting piously. 'And they mince along as they go, tinkling with their feet,' doing everything to be seen by men,* asking for every single step of their   *Cf. Mt 6:1*
feet only the reward of glory that will pass away.

5. The only cure for a vanity so manifold is humility, and even so, there has to be a copious and strong antidote for this ointment to overcome the infection of so great a poison. Hence, on this occasion, the spouse has good and fitting reason to begin his commendations at the feet. 'How beautiful', he says, 'are your feet in their sandals, O prince's daughter!'* Since, as scripture affirms, poison begins to creep stealthily from the soles of the feet right up to the crown of the head,* and so spreads its infection throughout the whole body, keeping it in a half-dead condition up to this present time, there neither is nor can be any cure for the sufferer until the pride has its foot lanced. Sickness climbs up from the foot, and from the same foot, the remedy for the sickness may find entrance. So the daughter of Zion, no longer savoring lofty matters, but sympathizing with things of no importance,* hears said to her: 'How beautiful are your feet in their sandals, O prince's daughter!'*

6. Now your feet have been endowed with full health, because now at last you have been persuaded to submit yourself to the grace of God. So now you can stand and walk, or rather, you can run and leap. You can stand, so as humbly to call down grace upon yourself by your prayers. You can walk, and advance your steps in justice, under the direction of grace. You can run, and, as grace increases, you can hasten your steps towards the end of the path, which is eternal life. You can leap, and come impetuously indeed, but happily, to the experience of those things

Sg 7:1

Cf. Is 1:6

Cf. Rm 12:16

Sg 7:1

which 'are above, with Christ',* for grace
bears you up. In all these circumstances,
'steps', that is, your spiritual progress, means
to stand, to rely on the grace of salvation, to
plead for grace from the Father of grace, and
this is truly to set your steps in heaven. To
turn somersaults with King David by leaping,
this is what is meant by walking among the
things of heaven.*

'How beautiful', he says, 'are your feet.'*
Of course, not as they were in days gone by,
when you went glancing wantonly, mincing
along and tinkling your feet,* when your
feet were still falsely and foolishly set on
human glory. But now, set down nobly and
truthfully, they are beautiful, for the sake of
God's glory. For 'charm is vain and beauty
deceitful'* when looked for in the empty
opinions of men and begged for with false
favors. But now that you are eager only to
please your spouse, you are beginning to show
the loveliness of total beauty, as far as your
feet are concerned, that is, by starting to be
humble.

7. But feet are twofold, consciousness of
our own weakness, and confidence in virtue.
In the path of life, one foot comes to help the
other with its mutual aid, so that, if one of
the two is in any way enfeebled, whether by
this foot trusting too much in itself, or the
other foot hoping too little in God, the soul
must of necessity go limping. Then she cannot
expect to hear these words of praise from the
spouse: 'How beautiful are your feet in their
sandals, O prince's daughter!'* But if, on the
contrary, the soul is sick in both feet,

Cf. Col 3:1

Cf. 2 S 6:16

Sg 7:1

Cf. Is 3:16

Pr 31:30

Sg 7:1

resembling the synagogue in the time of its sickness, and is completely unmindful of grace and does not recall her own sinfulness,* then she is very far indeed from these words of praise. Since she is not only unable to walk, but even unable to limp, she is all the more held down in the lonely bed of sickness.

Yet, all the same, her work is known to God,* though here on earth, she is seen to be lying prostrate, inglorious, sick, her whole body already almost dead. Still, in the eyes of that Majesty, to whom all things are equally present and nothing is still to come,* 'from the sole of her feet to the crown of her head',* there is no wound in her, no bruise or weal, 'no spot or wrinkle, or any such thing.'* To sum up, as Isaiah said: Here in this present age, he indeed hides his face from her for a little while, in a moment of wrath,* but very soon after, in his great compassions, she will be gathered to himself.*

8. With his characteristic tenderness then, the spouse himself will not withhold his heart, for she is like someone rising from her bed, after a very long sickness. No, forgetting immediately all her past offenses, he will run joyously to meet her. With a great cry of admiration, he will wipe away all tears from her eyes,* exclaiming, 'How beautiful are your feet in their sandals, O prince's daughter!'* It is as if he were to say: Your infirmities have been multiple, but now see what I have done! Not only are you made healthy, but your health too, is 'multiple'! For a long time, you were averted from me; at last, you have reverted to me; and now,

Cf. Ps 79:8

Cf. Ac 15:18

Cf. Heb 4:13

Is 1:16
Cf. Eph 5:27

Cf. Is 54:8

Cf. Is 54:7

Rev 7:17

Sg 7:1

you are wholly converted by me! With sudden and passionate swiftness, you have redeemed all you had lost by your wretched slowness. All that age-old blindness and stubbornness of yours has become for you what could be called a shortcut to salvation, a path of righteousness. All that obstinate hardness of heart of yours has become for you a barb urging to compunction and a spur to speed you forward. All that old impiety and blind pride of yours has become for you like a protection for your faith, like a new sandal for your new humility. Anything that you confess to having done in folly and wickedness, will not in future be a source of shame and a sign of your foolishness, but it will be a veil for your nakedness, an adornment of your beauty, a protection for your virtue.

The memory of all these things will be for you like the skins of dead animals, from which sandals are made for your humility. Humility in shoes will have no fear of the cold of laziness; the bites of serpents, that is, the deceits of evil spirits, will not frighten her. She will be undismayed by the different stones that obstruct her, namely, the trouble of any sort of trial, and she will not be soiled by any vanity through picking up the dust of earthly desires.

The example set by your forefathers, I mean the patriarchs and prophets, not to speak of the holy apostles, will in future be 'sandals' for your feet, sandals by no means thin or unworthy. You are now at last proving yourself their daughter by picking up their footprints and following them. Now

Cf. Gen 23:6

Jn 8:56

you are a true daughter of Abraham, who was called 'God's prince',* since you are doing the works of Abraham, having succeeded to his faith by hereditary right. He himself 'rejoiced to see my day,'* the day of his far distant descendant, and you have now become a partaker in this joy. You have already merited to 'see my day' through faith, and the time will come when you will eventually see it with your own eyes.

9. Taken in this sense, then, the humility of the synagogue is being commended for returning with great fervor to the ancient faith of her ancestors. At the very beginning of the path, her shame and repentance are welcomed by the tender-hearted spouse, not only to solace her by forgiveness, but also to praise her grace. But if, as the faith of the church believes, she immediately clothes herself in the virtue of preaching the gospel, so as to 'go about the city', as scripture says,* hungering for the salvation of all and burning with apostolic charity, then she will bring about a renewal of the mystery of the christian religion. It would be fitting, then, that she should be greeted by the voice of the spouse speaking to her in this manner: 'How beautiful are your feet in their sandals, O prince's daughter!'*

Cf. Sg 3:2

Sg 7:1

10. Isaiah is found using almost the same form of praise when he celebrates the primitive church by crying out in wonder: 'How beautiful on the mountains are the feet of those who bring the good news of peace, who bring news of good tidings.'* But in that case, it was the loveliness of the actual feet

Is 52:3

that was the wonder, while here it is the
beauty of the feet in movement. There it is
the quality of the preachers that has the
admiration, while here the praise goes to the
sandals. It is something not unlike this that
the apostle is declaring when he interprets the
meaning of 'sandal'. 'Sandaled feet', he says,
'are ready to preach the gospel of peace.'*   *Eph 6:15*
What is this 'readiness'? Surely it means that
everyone who is to have the duty of preaching the gospel, must be prepared to give
testimony to the Word of God in his own
blood, if need be? It means to proclaim
by the very quality of his life what he has
undertaken to proclaim by word of mouth
to give not the smallest offense, by word or
deed, to God's gospel, but to strive, whether
by life or by death,* for the Word of God to   *Cf. Ph 1:20*
'run and be glorified'.*   *Cf. 2 Thess 3:1*

Wearing sandals of this nature, the feet of
that early bride were beautiful indeed, and no
less beautiful will be the sandaled feet of this
modern bride. The holy and consecrated
thoughts of preachers are not soiled by the
dust of any earthly considerations, they halt
for no intimidation, they are shackled by no
attachment to flesh and blood, they are
caught up in no domestic anxieties. No, they
choose their way like a giant, and they rejoice
to run their race with giant strides.* A   *Cf. Ps 19:5*
double goad of charity drives them onwards,
for the love of their brothers' salvation urges
them on,* and an even more passionate love   *Cf. Rm 10:15*
for the glory of God's name urges them
still more.

Beautiful then are the feet of those who

Cf. Is 52:3

preach the gospel,* beautiful are their moving feet, for their heart is pure, their motive is untainted, their progress is as glorious to God as it is fruitful for the whole world.

11.   Again, when the spouse says, 'prince's daughter,' he could have two meanings. He may be restoring her to her nobility of birth, so that now, because of her faith, she deserves to be called daughter of Abraham,* as we discussed previously, and Abraham is undoubtedly, by God's decree, father of the prince of believers.* Or, he may be claiming for her an even nobler birth and calling her the daughter of that mighty prince who has undertaken to have the government laid upon his shoulder,* and become the prince of peace.* She has inherited his example, in so far as, being a true daughter of the prince, she too is ready to have the government of her Father laid upon her shoulder. In labor and distress, 'in hunger and thirst, in cold and nakedness,'* and in all the other perils of evangelizing, she seeks to reap the harvest of peace in God's church, so that she may herself become a prince of peace for all the children of peace.

12.   There still remains to be discussed, if the small compass of this sermon could support it, the manner in which these words can be applied to any soul. Tomorrow, then, God willing, you will get what you are waiting for, to your spiritual profit and to mine, if God wills it, to the praise and glory of the Son of God, spouse of the church, our Lord Jesus Christ, who with the Father and the Holy Spirit,

lives and reigns, God,
for ever and ever.
Amen.

SERMON SIXTY-FIVE

The beginning of the sixty-fifth sermon. What is meant by the feet, the footsteps, the sandals, the sandaled feet, of the soul who loves God. First, with regard to the soul whose duty it is to keep watch as a pastor, and then with regard to the soul who serves as a humble soldier in the service of Christ's charity, and finally, why a soul of this nature is called a prince's daughter.

'HOW BEAUTIFUL ARE YOUR FEET in their sandals, O prince's daughter!'* You have me in your debt, and here I am, to fulfill it! You are patiently waiting to hear something of spiritual profit about these words of praise, in which the spouse, rejoicing with his bride, begins to praise her in a new way. Not only does he graciously extol her feet, but he speaks of her sandals, too. Let us consider carefully, as far as we can, by the assistance of the same spouse, what is meant by 'the feet' of a soul who loves God, and what by her 'footsteps', her 'moving feet', and finally her 'feet in their sandals.'

2. As for the 'feet', which are the principal support of the soul who is well disposed, I think they are the two most important dispositions, by which I mean, love and hope. Clearly enough, if she is to be able to move

36

and advance towards her goal, the power of love must be at hand, divinely engrafted within her. But, since, by her own power, she is unable either to move or advance, and she is well aware of her own weakness, or rather, inability, she must, of necessity, through the power of hope, rely on the divine power. She must have a total distrust of herself, and she must lean with great confidence on God.

On these two feet, then, the soul that seeks Jesus walks the way of love, which Paul called 'the most excellent way,'* and which David describes as 'the way of God's testimonies', in which, he says, he delighted 'as in all riches.'* Moreover, to go in this way is to make good progress, and to have reached some new state through these dispositions, is to have imprinted new tracks on the road with her feet. In fact, anything marked with a sense of humility, through the foot of hope, or a sense of tenderness, through the foot of love, is clearly of profit to the traveler and shortens his way. This is why it is said to those who walk in the path of life: 'Every place on which your sandaled foot shall tread, shall be yours.'*

3. I beg you, in your charity, take good note of the phrasing of this promise, truly great, truly divine. 'Every place', it says, 'on which your sandaled foot shall tread, shall be yours.'* 'O, the voice of the Lord, preparing the stags!'* What room can there be for sluggishness or inactivity, when all justice, which is the true land of promise, flowing with milk and honey,* is set before us as something we can gain in no other way, buy

Cf. 1 Co 12:31

Ps 119:14

Dt 11:24

Ibid.
Ps 29:8

Ex 5:8

at no other price, than merely to walk over it with the steps of a holy desire, by hoping and by loving? Anywhere at all where we have once happened to be lovingly and reverently disposed, that place we have stamped as our own for all eternity. We have set our mark upon it, never to be destroyed for ages to come. Almost as if with an inscription of living characters and affixing a secret seal, we have claimed it for our own by hereditary right. Scripture tells us that this was first said to Abraham, and now all the heirs of the promise have the same said to them: 'Arise, walk through the length and breadth of the land, for I shall give it to you.'*

Indisputably it is charity, as the apostle says, that has precisely these two dimensions: it is patient and kind.* In its long-suffering, it has the 'length' of patience, and in its wide tolerance it has the 'breadth' of kindliness. So, anyone who has set his heart on becoming the heir of this great patriarch, will have to exercise himself continually in both these dimensions of charity. At one time he must walk over the promised land in its length, and at another in its breadth, and by imprinting the traces of a religious disposition at every step, he will add to his inheritance every place on which he sets his sandaled foot.*

4. And notice how, by a marvelous arrangement, the two dispositions we mentioned are set in motion. They act alternately, and when one is stationary, the other moves. As though by mutual help and love, one keeps itself behind so that the other can go in front. But the one that has now gone

in front, motivated by the same charity, submits itself to its companion and holds itself back for a moment, so as to give precedence to the other. In these holy dispositions, this is the unchangeable law that is solemnly laid down by the legislator, who is the author of charity, in other words, the Holy Spirit.

In fact, then, if the disposition of love is to be able to move forward, the hope of attaining its desire must, for the time being, press itself down, through humble trust in grace. If it did not, it would be altogether impossible, at the moment, to move forward the disposition of love. But, when hope has halted, love, moving forward by the step of tender affections, settles itself firmly in the way of divine charity, in order that the disposition of hope, assisted by love, may also, in the meantime, gain strength for some more effective enterprise. Obviously, if charity is not firmly settled, hope has no place, or better, no power, to set out, that is, to advance.

So then, 'feet' are the dispositions, 'footsteps' are the permanent states, and 'feet in movement' are each single step, that is, each advance. And beautiful indeed are these moving feet in the eyes of Him who sees the heart. The soul who is seeking God through loving desire, and hastening in its thirst to the fount of living waters,* takes so many steps, but none of them overhasty, is driven on by such swiftly moving feet, but all in order. The only condition is that love remembers to come to the help of hope, and hope of love, each in turn humbly and constantly assisting and supporting the other.

Cf. Jr 17:13

5. Consequently, since there is such a great length to this way, it is certainly a way, as scripture says, that is 'an eternal way,'* and since there is great height to this way, it is certainly an arduous and 'excellent way'.* The steps on it, then, are as if countless and untraceable, even for someone who is walking that very way.* To God alone is it right to say: 'You have searched out my paths and my destined way.'* To him alone is it right to confess, reverently: 'You have watched all my paths, you have set a bound to the tracks of my feet.'* Every single step our feet take leaves the sure and perpetual mark of its impress. It quickly slips away from us as we pass by, yet it has been written in our senses and scored deeply in our hearts by the finger of God. Moreover, even dogs, with their animal wisdom, follow invisible footprints once they have caught the scent. How much more will all these loving steps of our feet be wholly unable to hide from, quite unable to escape, the Wisdom of God, as he leads and guides them?

6. Again, the foot that we have called 'love', retains distinctly in God's eyes the proofs of its imprint, or of its perfume. It devotes itself to the good desire to be of service, whether in desire or joy or wonder or praise or thanksgiving to God, or entering into the joys and sufferings of others, encouraging them or rebuking them, consoling or giving some alms. At the same time, the foot we have called 'hope', leaves an equally clear trace of its imprint and its perfume, because in all its ways and paths, it stands firm

in the refusal to put no trust at all in its own wisdom and power. But this makes it cleave all the more wisely and strongly to God's wisdom and God's power. If it thinks it can do nothing without God,* it is just as convinced that in Him, it can do everything.* This is why it sings eagerly: 'Trusting in the Lord, I shall not be put to shame.'* And again: 'Since I have not known how to read the letters, I shall enter into the power of the Lord. O Lord, I proclaim your justice, yours alone!'*

Cf. Jn 15:5

Cf. Ph 4:13

Ps 26:1

Ps 71:12-13

O, how lovingly we can expect everything from God, when we expect nothing from ourselves! 'Since', says the psalmist, 'I have not known how to read the letters,' setting no store by my own knowledge, learning or experience, it is for this very reason that, freely and confidently, 'I shall enter into the power of the Lord.' There is nothing I cannot do in him, knowing as I do that there is nothing I can do without him. 'O Lord,' the psalm continues, 'I proclaim your justice, yours alone.' O cry of freedom, cry of faith! If my garments, he says, are like old rags that cannot cover or warm me,* or if they are like a woman's menstruous rags,* shaming rather than adorning me, still, 'I shall proclaim your justice, yours alone.'* I shall remember your justice, which is a new garment that never grows old, a warm garment, radiantly white which no crease wrinkles and no stain disfigures.*

Cf. 1 K 1:1

Est 14:16

Ps 71:14

Cf. Eph 5:27

So, the 'foot of love' leaves the traces of devotion and fervor, while the 'foot of hope' inscribes the marks of humility and confidence on the mind of the soul that loves God.

7. But there is some great significance in the 'sandals', which the spouse admires on his bride's feet. In fact, it is her feet when sandaled that receive his commendation. 'How beautiful', he says, 'are your feet in their sandals, O prince's daughter!'* These are certainly not the kind of sandal that Moses was once told to take off his feet,* but neither are they the kind that the disciples were forbidden to wear when they were sent out to preach the gospel.* In both these cases, the burden of earthly cares is to be laid aside, because the holy ministry of the Word of God is to be taken up. The feet of those who preach must be unencumbered, and no domestic anxieties, concerned with things that perish, ought to involve or burden men whose duty is to proclaim heavenly and eternal realities.

Nevertheless, it is certainly not permissible for them to go barefoot, since they have been ordered to have 'their feet shod with the preparation of the gospel of peace.'* The ministry of preaching and pastoral care, then, is a completely new kind of sandal, one that is specially made for the feet of those who truly bring the news of Christ, and who, in their pastoral duties, are not seeking what is their own, but what is Jesus Christ's.* On the other hand, though, those who are under the influence of their own spirit and are not sent out by the Holy Spirit, men who come, not to serve, but to be served,* for these there is neither part nor inheritance in these words of praise: 'How beautiful are your feet in their sandals, O prince's daughter!'*   *Sg 7:1*

Let men like this listen, covered with shame and confusion, to what Isaiah says. He passed them by, and called out admiringly to men of true glory: 'How beautiful on the mountains are the feet of those who preach goodness.'*   *Is 52:7*   Then Paul tells us that this 'beauty of their feet' means that they preach because they are sent, not taking the honor to themselves, but called by God, as Aaron was.*   *Rm 10:15*   'How are they to preach,' he says, 'unless they are sent?'*   *Rm 10:15*   And then he adds on beneath: 'As it is written: How beautiful are the feet of those who preach the gospel of peace.'*   *Cf. Is 52:7*   So this sending, by the Holy Spirit, puts sandals on the feet of pastors, or of the Lord's bride, 'in preparation' for the salvation of their brothers;*   *Cf. Eph 6:15*   in other words, it gives weight and equipment to the dispositions.

8. It gives weight, because the bride, holding in her hands the price entrusted to her, namely, the Lord's blood, is not allowed to slumber or to sleep.*   *Ps 121:3*

As if she is now shod in new sandals, she hears said to her: 'Go, hasten, importune your neighbor, give no sleep to your eyes and let not your eyelids slumber!'*   *Pr 6:3,4*   It gives dignity, for, as the apostle tells us, 'those who serve well, gain a good standing for themselves, and great confidence, which is in Christ Jesus.'*   *1 Tm 3:13*

How happy the soul is who waits, patiently and trustfully, for the end of time, when Jesus will utter the 'Well done!' of honor and glory! And while he waits, she manfully shuts

Cf. Pr 6:17

her ear to 'the deceitful tongues',* that try to overwhelm her with vainglory and weave snares for her from the good opinions she hears both within and without. They are ever

Mt 25:21

whispering to her: Well done, well done!*

So any soul who is truly the Lord's bride, will remember, day and night, what weight and dignity have come to her in her acceptance of these 'sandals'. But since she has no desire to hoard it up for no purpose, she never stops paying it out, as we described above, by constantly traveling around either to or on behalf of those to whose service she is dedicated. For these sandals are not consumed by age or worn out by any use, rather, that use only means they become more honored and valued.

The bride is aware that she is responsible for the wise, but even more for the foolish, if her feet in their sandals are to give the prince pleasure. Indeed, she looks on the foolish with all the indulgence of a mother's tenderness, and repeats with her spouse: 'Over Edom

Ps 60:8

I shall cast my shoe.'* What she means is this: Over my little ones, still only wise in the things of this world and the things of the flesh, I shall cast a generous measure of the concern they need. I shall show favor to them very willingly, I shall show myself very understanding. Of course, I have the example of the

Jn 11:14

good, the unique Shepherd,* so that I cannot disregard that I am bound more strongly to the weaker sheep. It is to seek out the lost and to strengthen the enfeebled that I know I was specially sent. It was for this that the Lord shod me in sandals, this above all.

Any soul that feels like this, and stands, keeping guard over his charge,* eager for the salvation of the sheep entrusted to her, zealous for God's glory alone, and not for his own, that soul has glory, and God will reveal it in heaven when the time comes. That soul has no fear of hearing the eternal condemnation, and of her house being called 'house of one who has no sandals'.* No, her dwelling will be with those who build for themselves houses in heaven, not made with hands,* to one of whom the Lord promised: 'I myself shall build you a house that will last.'*   *Cf. Is 21:8*

Dt 25:10

Cf. Mk 14:58

1 K 11:38

9. However, if this soul also is to have a right to await, with the bride, these spoken words of praise, and hear, just as she does, 'How beautiful are your feet in their sandals, O prince's daughter!',* then she will have to rival the movement of the bride's sandaled feet. By this I mean, she will have to imitate her progress very carefully. Accordingly, the 'movement of the bride's sandals' is, at one time to go out to look after the maidens, at another time to go back again to see to oneself, and lastly—and this is what is most important—to go in to contemplate the spouse. 'Who among all is as faithful as David,' says scripture, 'going in and coming out, on the king's service?'* But perhaps the bride has an even higher merit than being 'faithful', because her desire is not only to go forward for her neighbor's benefit, and make humble progress for her own sake, but she also strives, gracefully and passionately, to go out of herself into her spouse.   *Sg 7:1*

1 S 22:14

It may be that someone reading or listening

to this may object that these commendatory
words are being taken too exclusively as
meaning those who undertake the pastoral
office. There may be a feeling it is time
this 'shoe' was also 'cast over'* those who
have learned humble submission. This expectation finds an immediate answer in the
meaning we have given to 'sandals', because
some of the saints have thought that these
sandals symbolized feats of holy mortification or the commands that God has laid down.
Taken in that sense, the disciples are forbidden to carry sandals,* in case they weigh
themselves down with the deadly customs
and examples of wicked men. Moreover,
when they ate the lamb, they were ordered to
'have sandals on their feet',* to protect them
with the religious practices of their pre-
decessors.

10. According to this meaning, then, this
message of salvation is specially sent to you,
dearest brothers.* For you consent to have
your feet, that is, your disposition, con-
strained by very tight sandals, namely, by the
example given by your fathers, and by their
rule of life. Perhaps, to some of you, all this
seemed hard and painful, to those who are just
beginning and are, as it were, taking their
first steps. It may have felt as if they had put
your foot into a fetter and that they already
felt you were imprisoned.* But, all the same,
they patiently endured the experience of their
early days, for they had heard that it is a
strict way 'that leads to life,'* and they
accepted the restraints of the present in the
hope of future freedom. And that hope did

not disappoint them, either, for, 'it is good
to wait quietly for the salvation of God.'*   *Lam 3:26*

Even now, we see with joy, and relate it
happily, that this hard way of God's commandments, on which they embarked so
fearfully and began, all crawling and halting,
trying to walk rather than succeeding,
now they can walk it, upright and confi-
dent. In fact, they can now even run along it,
setting their feet down strongly and regularly.
But beginners, to some extent, fear even a
word, a gesture or a nod, that will lead them
to stumble against some tiny little 'stone of
offense'.* Yet, to all such timorous souls, so   *Cf. Is 8:14*
careful about every step, could it not be said
by the Holy Spirit: 'God has given his angels
charge of you, to keep you in all your ways'?*   *Is 90:9*

Surely, feet are 'beautiful in their sandals'
when they are the feet of one who places
herself under the authority of superiors and
models herself on the noble example of her
equals? One who is careful 'in all her ways' to
see how to offend no one by her own example
and to conform herself to the example of
others? How beautiful are such 'feet in their
sandals', saved from the grime of peculiarity
by their imitation of others, and protected
from spiritual cowardice by the example of so
many forebearers and companions. They are
beautiful indeed, bound, as if in tight sandals,
by the need to obey and the discipline of
religious life in common, and yet, at the same
time, free choice and chosen freedom make
them free and unconstrained.* Yes, they are   *Cf. Bernard,*
beautiful, given over to the good of the   *Gra 3.7;*
church, through their love for their brothers,   *SBOp 3:171;*
                                                   CF 19:63.

and yet, 'how beautiful they are', when the depths of their heart is disposed to please God and behold the angels.

11. Any soul like this is well described as 'the prince's daughter', because freely, to please God, she has bound herself in this unavoidable captivity, and this makes her truly the daughter of the truly free Jesus. He did not come to do his own will, but the will of him who sent him,* and it was this that brought him by right, the principality of everlasting lordship and the glory of that name 'which is above every name.'* In his great love, he has kept a share in that name for his daughter, as she moves and points her 'feet in their sandals'. In the measure that she now strives to be the ruler over all her land, in other words, tries to control all her desires and dispositions, so, when Christ's glory is revealed, will the prince's daughter become heir to her father and share in his principality.

'Lift up your gates, you princes',* lift up your head, anyone of you who feels you are 'a prince's daughter', because 'your principality is greatly strengthened'.* Although, on this earth, it has been hidden from your own eyes, take courage, because the time is near when it will be revealed. In a very little while, O prince's daughter, 'your principality will be upon your shoulder',* because an eternal weight of glory will be laid upon you by your Father, the Prince of princes, as much as your shoulder can carry.* Instead of the weight, heavy and yet passing, which here on earth the charity of Christ has made light,* you will receive that weight, itself heavy, and

yet light and glorious, never to be shaken off
your shoulder; may it be kept there by him
who gave it, Our Lord, the Father's only Son,
who with the same Father
and the Holy Spirit,
lives and reigns,
God, for ever
and ever.
Amen.

The beginning of the sixty-sixth sermon. How 'the joining of the bride's thighs' symbolizes the charity which, on the last day, will make her solicitous for two communities, namely, the circumcised and the uncircumcised, anxious to unite them in the same bond of faith and charity, through the assistance of the greatest of craftsmen, the Holy Spirit.

'THE JOINING OF YOUR THIGHS is like a necklace, work of a master craftsman.'*

Sg 7:1

In the last verse, it was the Shulamite's feet, beautiful in her sandals, that the spouse admired, and we interpreted this as meaning the humility, and also the devotion, of his new bride, the synagogue, when she is, at the last, converted. She will be repentant at the length of time it took to convert her, and she will clothe herself in a firm resolution to preach the gospel, because she hopes, in this way, to be more fully reconciled to her husband, having herself become the reconciliation of 'the full number of the gentiles'.* When those last days come, the loving faith of holy church will expect something great and indescribable from this conversion, first because of the promises of the prophets, then from fresh promises of the apostles, and finally

Rm 11:25

from these proclamations of the spouse about
which we are at present engaged.

2. Without any doubt, there are multiple
predictions by the prophets that, at the end
of time, the bride will seek for her former
husband,* for her King David.† And again: *Cf. Hos 2:7
'If the number of the sons of Israel is as the   †Cf. Hos 3:5
sand of the sea, a remnant will return from
them.'* And Isaiah also says: 'A remnant will   Is 10:22
return, a remnant of Jacob, to the mighty
God, in truth.'* How great will be the fruit of   Is 10:21
this return, and how great its perfection, we
learn from the joyful testimony of this same
prophet: 'The destruction that is decreed, will
overflow with righteousness.'* When Paul   Is 10:22
thought of these predictions, he seemed as if
brimming over with the oil of gladness.* He   Cf. Ps 45:7
raised his eyes to the solemn grandeur of
those days and cried aloud: 'If their trespass
means riches for the world, and their failure
means riches for the gentiles, how much more
will their full inclusion mean?'* And a little   Rm 11:12
later: 'If their rejection means the reconciliation of the world, what will their acceptance
mean but life from the dead?'*   Rm 11:15

3. It was the spouse who, through the
mouths of the prophets and apostles, splendidly inaugurated the praises of his future
wife, and through the same mouths he brings
them to completion. And now, he opens his
own mouth to enumerate the steps she will
take in the so distant future, and to describe,
one by one and in careful order, every item of
her sweet, new manner of living. So, after he
has mentioned that she has sandals on her
feet, 'in preparation for the gospel of peace,'*   Eph 6:15

Cf. Sg 7:1

Eph 4:3

Cf. Eph 4:4

Cf. 2 Tm 4:3

Cf. Ps 58:3

Gal 4:11

Gal 4:19

he readily praises the 'joining of the thighs',* meaning by this, her care to preserve unity in the bond of peace.*

Yes, it is the great and foremost care of those who preach the gospel of eternal peace, to bind together in the same charity of spirit those whom they have brought into the christian faith. They are to be the one body of Christ, one spirit in Christ, just as they were called in one hope of their calling.* Otherwise, how will it help anyone to be conceived within the womb of the church by faith, if the growth does not receive its form from charity? Speaking of those who are led away by false apostles and desert wholesome teaching,* who begin to go astray from the womb and to wander in falsehood from their birth,* the apostle says with groans and reproaches: 'I am afraid I have labored over you in vain.'* And a little further on: 'My little children, with whom I am again in travail until Christ be formed in you.'*

You can see, I think, 'the joining of the thighs' in this loving mother, and I am referring to Paul's charity. Here, not without indescribable spiritual pleasure, he conceived for Christ so noble and so numerous a family, but all the same, it was not without great interior pain, and sighs and groans, that he gave it birth.

4. But since the thigh is an apt symbol for spiritual generation, the 'joining of the thighs' is obviously an expression of the holy union of Jews and gentiles in the faith of Christ. These two walls are very far removed from each other, but in Christ Jesus, 'the corner

stone',* they meet at right angles. To the in-   *Eph 2:20*
finite joy of heaven and earth, through the
great labors of preachers, there arises from
these walls one city of God the all-powerful,
built with hard toil but also with the wisdom
of a master-craftsman. Hence the words: It
rises to give joy to the whole earth, Mount
Zion, far in the north, the great king's city.'*   *Ps 48:2*
Yes, he is indeed, a 'great king', Christ Jesus,
very great and worthy of all praise, and Mount
Zion, like a great city that is far too small and
inadequate, cannot correspond with his greatness, without including 'the far north,'*   *Ibid.*
which means the full tally of the gentiles.

5. So it is said 'to the north: give up; and
to the south: do not withhold.'* And at   *Is 43:6*
God's command, the north did adopt a more
gentle spirit. It spread out to the noonday
sun its far-off regions and melted with south-
ern warmth the hardened ice of the ages,
for the Holy Spirit restored it from its captivity,* like a stream flowing swiftly in the   *Cf. Ps 126:1*
south.* But the south, that was commanded   *Cf. Ps 125:5*
not to withhold, disobeyed the Holy Spirit.
It breathed against the north the fire of its
envy, it conspired against it with all its power,
and it hardened its face against it until, 'far in
the north', the south too should set its
throne,* because the coldness of its unbelief   *Cf. Is 12:14*
had stiffened into ice the tenderness of faith.
Moreover, the heat of its envy made it 'a boiling pot'* to attack the trustfulness of the   *Cf. Jr 1:13*
gentiles.

Consequently, it was pride, 'root of all
evils',* that produced this flame of unquench-   *1 Tm 6:10*
able envy. Because God had given it a distinc-

Cf. Rm 1:3

tive form of worship, Israel 'according to the flesh'* presumed to triumph even more over the blindness of the gentiles. But the blow struck by this pride inflicted on it the wound of the gentiles, since it was swelling up against God, as if in virtue of its special dignity and justice, when it grew arrogant, in its contempt for the gentiles he had not chosen. It was puffed up against the justice of God, who had chosen it out of all nations to receive the full gift of faith. It was inflamed against the unhappiness of the gentiles, feeling no religious pity for their blindness, but only irreligious anger. So, in one case they were haughty and inflated through their arrogance, and in the other, they were wholly irreligious and abusive through their contempt.

6. Here were two roots from which there sprouted a two-fold envy; Zion hated that the gentiles either should receive or had received illumination. Indeed, as the apostle tells us, she forbade the apostles to preach the word of salvation to the gentiles,* and when they had preached it, she was furious that they had brought it to an 'uncircumcised nation'.* I repeat, as far as was in her power, the south forbade any preacher to give the word of faith to the north and, equally, forbade the north to give any of her preachers faith in the Word.

So the two of them, jew and gentile, stood there before the tribunal of eternal justice, with God sitting in judgement, and Israel, with that twofold pride we have spoken of, and that twofold envy, gave God his answer.

It was only because she alone presumed to
glory that she alone was thrust away from
God, and it was only because she alone
sneered at the poverty of the gentiles that
only she herself became poverty-stricken. She
was jealous that they should receive light, and
so she herself became blinded by the same
light. Without compassion, she withheld from
them what has now been done, to her cruel
anguish. But the supreme and eternal kind-
ness which God* showed to those who, as it   *Cf. 1 P 2:10*
is written, were at one time not his people,
has never ceased to be a provocation to them,
for such is the incurable rage of this poison,
to waste away at the sight of goodness, to be
savage in the face of kindness, to rage at
mercy, to groan when others exult and to
feel pain when others are saved.

7. Scripture tells us that the most loving
of fathers had an older son, and that, when he
heard the singing and dancing of those who
were making merry over the return of his
younger brother, he refused pointblank to go
and join them.* Even when his father pressed   *Cf. Lk 15:28*
him to come in, he preferred to remain alone
outside, eaten up with spiteful distress, rather
than take his place inside among the happy
guests, all united in rejoicing.* To this very   *Lk 15:25*
day, the tender Father waits, as delighted
by the restoration of the prodigal son as he is
anxious to bring home the son who still stands
outside the door.* Although the wound   *Cf. Lk 15:28*
seems incurable, he soothes it with ointment
he has carefully compounded, by pointing out
how closely related are the names, 'brother'
and 'son'. He brings this relationship to mind

and urges upon him the feeling of natural loyalty which ought to make him show a brother's reactions to his brother's return. The apostles, in their day, imitated this heavenly goodness. As if by a skillful 'joining of their thighs',* they set themselves to be in labor with both these peoples and bring them to birth in God. Although so many were brought to birth, there was to be no question of one nation being supplanted by the other or being held back.*

8. How many are the arguments, and how strong and how subtle, with which the apostle represses the pride of both people. First there was the pride of the gentiles, to whom the apostle was appointed 'in faith and truth.'* He pointed out the arrogance that arose from boasting in the teachings of philosophy,* which was therefore condemned by the true Wisdom and abandoned to the many different errors of idolatry.* He showed how their pride was all covered over with the dirt of shame and disgrace.* Then he reproached Israel, presenting herself in the flesh with immense authority because of her recognition of God and the works of the law. But she took no notice of God's justice and preferred to set up her own, scorning to submit to the justice of God.* So now, through their own fault, they have fallen over the stumbling block.*

Then, when the pride of both has been exposed and completely shattered, he recalls them both to christian humility and, in the peace of Christ, he binds together under the one yoke of faith, the humbled necks of them both.

9. It is in the apostles that the prophecy
of Isaiah finds fulfillment: 'Happy are you
who sow beside all waters, who bind together
the feet of the ox and the ass.'* He said 'all   *Is 32:20*
waters', meaning, all the apostles; the 'seed' is
the word of God; the 'feet of ox and ass' is
the disposition of both people, humbled by
their long alienation from God. Clearly, this
sign of their humiliation provided the oppor-
tunity for them to come together in unity
and agree together on the same form of
peace. They had been enticed in different
ways by the aberrations of pride, and now
the unifying loyalty of the faith has bound
them into one.

There must be no chance for one side to
glory at the expense of the other, either by
vaunting their own justice or inconsiderately
mocking at the justice of the other.* To   *Cf. 1 Co 4:6*
prevent it, the apostle unveiled very completely the infidelity and sinfulness of both
groups, as we said before, recalling that 'everything is under the power of sin',* so that 'the   *Cf. Rm 3:9*
whole world may be accountable to God.'*   *Rm 3:19*
This, of course, is the chain holding them
together, that binds equally 'the foot of ox
and ass',* this is the 'joining of the bride's   *Is 32:20*
thighs',* this is the 'necklace made by a   *Cf. Sg 7:1*
master at his craft',* namely, the intricate   *Ibid.*
fastening of this holy union. The craftsman
of it all, as we said above, is the Holy Spirit,
who, in a wonderful and delicate manner, has
taken pride and fashioned it into humility.
Out of faithlessness he has fashioned faith,
out of darkness, light, out of superstition,

truth, producing unity out of all this diversity.

10. But there are two ways in which this 'joining of the thighs' or this precious and intricate necklace can be seen. This is whenever a nation apostatizes from the faith, and another takes its place as faithful believers, or whenever, through the teaching of the apostles, as I have described, and by the assistance of the Holy Spirit, they all meet together as one in the unity of the faith. This is what we read happened in the early church, after the ascension of Christ into heaven, to the great joy of the whole assembly,* and we await its coming in even fuller fashion at the end of the world, as if in the autumnal richness of the harvest. But as for the first 'joining', in which one of them seems to have incurred blindness in such a manner that it yields illumination to the other, that is a joining so skilled and marvelous that it seems beyond the power of the mind of man to understand it.

Cf. Ac 2:46

11. But the apostle asserts with wonder that such, in actuality, was this 'joining', and he wonders at his assertion. For he says, when he is proclaiming the message to the gentiles: 'Just as you were once unbelievers, but now have received mercy because of their unbelief,' that is, the children of Israel, 'so now they have become unbelievers, so that, by the mercy shown to you, they also may receive mercy.'* And, explaining in some measure, the reason for this mystery: 'For God', he says, 'has consigned all men to disobedience, that he may have mercy upon all.'*

Rm 11:30,31

Rm 11:32

But this 'reason' is in itself also a most profound mystery, namely, how the spouse can be so restricted in his position that he is forced to cut off one out of the two. It may be that the apostle has a reverent dread of what he himself is not able to comprehend, or perhaps it is that he chose not to reveal it to us, but anyway, he has taught us to reverence and adore the mystery of it, crying out in his fear: 'O the depth of the riches and wisdom and knowledge of God! How unsearchable are his judgements and how inscrutable are his ways!'* *Rm 11:33*

12. Unsearchable these depths may be, yet the same apostle lets down his nets to make a catch, and shows us how we can use them to see more deeply into God's kindness and severity. 'See', he says, 'the severity and kindness of God.'* In other words, for those who *Rm 11:22* fall, severity, but for you, who stand fast in the faith, goodness, as long as you remain in goodness. Naturally, since the honor of God loves just dealing,* his power and severity, *Cf. Ps 99:4* always accompanied by wisdom and justice, are not able to enlighten his human creatures except from the very light of his judgements.* *Cf. Rm 1:20* It pleases him that these very judgements should be working in turn among the circumcised and then the uncircumcised, and at one and the same time, he wants to make a generous grant of the riches of his goodness to one side from the very fact of its being rejected by the other.

When we think of the vocation of the gentiles, which of us is not far more overcome with amazement and moved far more deeply to give thanks for God's goodness, by the act of comparing that same goodness with the severity that gave a bill of divorce to the earlier wife?* It is into her joys that he has brought the lowly born and shapeless Ethiopian.* So the new bride has a new token of her new love from her new spouse, and that is a memorial of infinite goodness itself, which is wonderfully emphasized both by his former unworthiness and his repudiation of his first bride. But that first bride also once had a necklace of the same kind from her spouse, because, before her, all the nations were in his presence as if they never existed,* and the portion of his inheritance fell to Jacob's lot alone.* The hands of the same craftsman making use of this time of her desolation, are fashioning a necklace no less precious for her, even if she is for the moment divorced, and his long enduring severity and goodness, poured out at the end of time will delicately put the finishing touch with a cunning link.

13. Moreover, the joining, namely, the union that is made of the two people through the preaching of his name, will result not in one necklace, but in a double string of beads. This means that 'Ephraim, as scripture puts it,' will not be jealous of Judah,'* nor Judah of Ephraim, that is, the circumcised and the uncircumcised will not be tormented with envy over their common vocation. On the contrary, mercy and truth will greet each other* with loving rejoicing. Truth is what the apostle assigns to the house of Israel, in confirmation of the promises made to their fathers, and 'it is for the gentiles', he says, 'to glorify God for his mercy.'*

To conclude, this joining of the thighs of
the bride, by her twin labors in converting
both people to the faith, will implant in the
lap of either a suitable ornament, fashioned
by the hand of a craftsman, her spouse: this
will serve as a reminder to preserve more faithfully both charity and chastity towards their
spouse and mutual charity towards one another.

For deciding this, and feeling such compassion, glory and honor be to the only
Son of God, the church's spouse,
our Lord Jesus Christ, who,
together with the Father
and the Holy Spirit,
lives and reigns,
God, for ever
and ever.
Amen.

SERMON SIXTY-SEVEN

The sixty-seventh sermon. How the 'joining of the thighs' of the bride is the sign of a wonderful concord in the church between kingly power and priesthood. The prophet Zechariah shows them in symbol, the royal power in Zerubbabel and the priesthood in Joshua, son of Josedech, and prophesies that the house of God, that is, the church, is to be raised up by the policy of one as much as of the other.* But the two powers, as one in Melchisedech* and now in the pope, reveal the form of him who is true king and true priest.

'THE JOINING OF YOUR THIGHS is like a necklace, work of a master craftsman.'*

In the previous sermon, we ascribed the 'joining of the bride's thighs' to the mystery of the love between the circumcized. Scripture tells us that, in the early days of the growing church, the apostles worked at this charity, and we believe that the heirs to the grace of the apostles are to work at it till the end of time.* But there are all the ages in between, when the church is receiving strength and sustenance from the Spirit of her spouse. We must not leave them unaccounted for and seem to be depriving her of her necklace. The spouse says it is 'the work of a master craftsman', and full attention must be paid to this aspect, too.

2. The 'joining of her thighs', then, can be quite justly applied to the union of power and priesthood. Obviously, the hiddenness of this union is holy and joyous, as fruitful in off-spring as it is pleasurable in its peacefulness. This is a union that has stretched wide the bounds of the christian faith, and an infinite fruitfulness has come forth from it, because of this 'joining of the thighs'. There is no end to the bringing forth of children while the pleasure of this peacefulness goes on in its abundance, to the bride's satisfaction. More-over, the spouse, as the source of this peace and the preserver equally of the dignity of king and priest, shines brightly in glory. He has the fulness of both consecrations and displays the banners of both authorities.*

Cf. Bernard, Ep 244.1; SBOp 8:134.

3. Clearly, these are the two lamb's horns, which John, in the Book of Revelations, saw on the lamb's forehead.* This is the twofold power of Zerubbabel, the great champion, and Joshua, the great priest, by whose joint strength and united policy Zechariah says the house of the Lord is to be rebuilt.* In reference to Zerubbabel, it is written in scripture: His 'hands have laid the foundation of this house, and his hands will complete it.'* And in the same prophecy, it says of Joshua, the great priest: 'He will build a house for the Lord, and it is he who will raise the Lord's temple.'* He will build, says the prophet, and he will raise, meaning that he will begin and bring to completion. When this same prophet discusses more fully this double

Cf. Rv 13:11

Ez 5:2

Zc 4:9

Zc 6:12

Zc 6:13

Cf. Zc 4:14

Zc 4:7

Cf. Ps 89:10

Zc 14:20

Cf. Dn 2:47

power of Christ, he says: 'There will be peaceful understanding between these two,'* Zerubbabel and Joshua, in other words, between royal authority and the priesthood. He prophesies that it is these two sons of anointing who have the right to stand by the Ruler of the whole earth,* which means he is calling them the men who establish the church in peace.

4. Of Zerubbabel, that is, of Christ's kingly glory, the prophecy runs that he will level a great mountain before him, 'and he will pull out the keystone and from its grace, take the level of grace.'* Thanks be to God, for a long time the church has had the joy of knowing that what was prophesied so many ages ago, was fulfilled in the kingship of her spouse. Obviously, the 'great mountain' is the power of the persecutors and the mad fury of despotic rulers, panting with all their might to destroy the name of Christ and raging against the church with every kind of agonizing death. At the command of the Lord, whose kingly power treads down the waves of the sea,* the mountain begins suddenly to subside and become level.

Indeed, even kings who have humbly accepted the holy christian faith, have the bridle of evangelical rule laid upon their necks by Christ. Just as we find it in this same prophecy, so it must be that 'upon the bridles of the horse, it is written: Holy to the Lord.'* For Christ Jesus is the king of kings,* and he holds curbed at his feet the regal power of these kings. With the bridle of his government, he begins to drive and lead them around at his own good pleasure, and through them, he bridles the nations they subdue and puts them under gospel government. Through the mouth of these kings, there issued a new edict from our Zerubbabel and our Augustus, the great king, in opposition to the savage edicts of the ancient despots, and it decreed that the whole world was to be enrolled in a new census of the christian faith.* *Cf. Lk 2:1*

So, the warhorse, namely, the might of kings, which once came down into the plain, snorting with rage* 'against the Lord and his anointed,'* received with trembling neck the mastery of the Lord who sits upon him and the bridle of his control, for fear of judgement to come. But, 'upon the horse's bridle, there is written: Holy to the Lord,'* because, in a wonderful way, the bridle of slaves, which fear first laid upon the horse, is charged into a holy thing by freely chosen devotion. They only truly begin to be free when Christ bestows on them his own freedom,* and they are only truly made kings again, when Christ, the King of kings, takes them into his own service. *Cf. Jb 39:24* *Ps 2:2* *Zc 14:20* *Cf. Gal 4:31*

5. And so, our Zerubbabel 'has pulled out the keystone',* which means he has shown the glory of his authority, through these kings. Also, with that stone, he has ground to powder the statue that Nebuchadnezzar saw,* namely, the illusory glory of this present world, which is really nothing but a fleeting apparition, a dream. He plays with kings and the great ones of the earth as if in sleep, reducing their glory to the dust of a summer's threshing floor.* In fact, at the *Cf. Zc 4:7* *Cf. Dn 2:31* *Cf. Dn 2:35*

radiant glory of the eternal king, all the
shadowy and unreal glory of this world
vanishes away, reduced to nothingness. This
is clear to the eyes that are not blinded* by
the dust of the summer's threshing floor, for
it has been blown away by the Holy Breath
of God.

Yes, the religion of blind idol-worship has
been ground to powder and shattered to
pieces, that religion which gloried in having
been set up, in satanic arrogance, to rival the
true God and destroy the world. With
unspeakable boldness, the devil claimed for
himself the glory of the name of God,* even
after 'the Word was made flesh.'* More: he
claimed that even after, he did not hesitate
to incur the guilt of God's death; even after,
he was unwilling that the resurrection and
ascension of the Son of God should make that
Son sit in glory at the right hand of the
Father. So he never fears being the champion
of the false religion he has established.
Through the swords of tyrants, he has gone
on fighting, inflicting the most inhuman
tortures on the saints. He has not shrunk
in his madness from crucifying Christ anew,
in so many thousands of martyrs.

But in all this, blind cunning and false
courage was advancing the cause of true Wisdom and true courage, though ignorantly and
unwillingly. In fact, the devil achieved the
world's salvation by the cross of the Son of
God, and when Christ emptied himself, the
devil was a wonderful instrument in his glori-
fication. By killing the martyrs, he wove their
crowns for them and brought a very rich

Cf. Jb 17:7

Cf. Mt 3:9
Jn 1:14

increase to Christ's glory on earth as well as in heaven. Furthermore, at the time fixed by his good pleasure, the Lord had only to breathe,* and the wild gale of his frenzy turned to a gentle breeze.* Lilies were exchanged for roses, and the righteousness of the martyrs was succeeded by overflowing peace.* He who showed himself to be 'God the strong'* in the steady faith of the martyrs, became 'the Prince of peace'* in the tranquility of the devout.

Cf. Ps 147:18

Cf. Mk 4:39

Cf. Ps 72:7

Cf. Ps 7:12

Cf. Is 9:6

So the keystone was pulled out to crush the worship of devils and proclaim the worship of God, to sweep away the glory of the world and manifest the glory of God.

6. However, the words that come next: 'from its grace, take the level of grace,'* refer to the glory of Christ the king. It is his right freely to bestow the grace of royal splendor on whom he chooses and to the extent he chooses. It is for him to reward that grace with some new grace, and in the end, it is for him to set the crown on every grace, for he has either freely taken the first step in it, or he has spontaneously increased it, or he has granted the gift of the beatific vision. This last grace is both the supreme bestowal of glory and the reward of every other grace, so that it is in itself simultaneously the loveliest of all graces and a grace that is completely free and supereminent. This is why it is expressly with reference to this final grace that the psalmist trusts in God for all his soul needs, saying, 'He crowns you with mercy and compassion.'*

Zc 4:7

Ps 103:4

So much for the kingly power of Christ.

Zc 6:11

Zc 6:12-14

Sg 7:1

7. But when it comes to the priestly office, the same prophet we have already quoted, is commanded, by the Lord's command, to take silver and gold from the princes who came out of Babylon in the transmigration, and to make crowns with it and place them on the head of Joshua, son of Josedech, the great priest.'* The prophet is to say to him: 'The Lord of power and might says this: 'Here is a man whose name is Branch, where he is, there will be a branching out, and he will build the temple of the Lord. It is he who will raise up the Lord's temple; it is he who will bear the royal honor and sit and rule upon his throne. And a priest will be his throne, and peaceful understanding will be between them both. And the crown will be in the Lord's temple, a memorial to Heldai, Tobijah, Jedaiah, and to Josiah, the son of Zephaniah.'*

I may seem to have quoted these words of the prophet at rather great length, but the wonderful 'joining of the bride's thighs',* which can be seen shining out from these words, as if from a glimmering cloud, is something I confess to finding very moving. Or, better still, it is the love of Christ's glory, so unmistakably expressed in this passage, that I find moving. What could be more unmistakable, than for the holy name of Jesus, or Joshua, to be found in both image and reality? But, for even greater clarity, the great priest is also described as 'the son of Josedech', a name that is translated as 'Lord of justice'. Quite obviously, this points most directly to the Father of our Lord Jesus

Christ. But although these names, as I have said, are common to both, the shadow and the light, the symbol and what is symbolized, something unique, a name shared by no other is added, for the prophet says, 'Behold, a man whose name is "Rising" '.*   *Zc 6:12*

8. O name of glory! O name 'which is above every name!'* This name is a name that speaks of Christ's birth from eternity, for the Lord Jesus, who was 'rising' before time began, has never ceased to be 'risen', and he never will cease, to the end of the ages. But his begetting is a begetting that cannot be described; just as it has no beginning, so neither has it an end. Even among the angels, who can speak about it, or rather, who is there, who can even think about it worthily, as it is in itself? This is surely why it is said to Christ by his Father, in the psalm: 'The Lord said to me: "You are my Son, today I have begotten you."*' 'The Lord' says to me, as if saying 'the Son' is the only one able to grasp the meaning as if he is the only one who can be thought worthy of speaking about the mystery of so great a secret, whether to man or angel. 'It is I', he says, 'who have begotten you this day.' By the 'day' of eternity, he indicates a changeless present. And when he says, 'I begot you', he expresses a fullness of begetting, in its totality.   *Ph 2:9*   *Ps 2:7*

Also, besides this, since the only Son of the Father 'stooped to be born of the virgin, his name is Rising,'* as we can see those words of the psalm, with their fresh note of wonder: 'Truth has risen forth from the earth.'*   *Zc 6:12*   *Ps 2:7*

But even if no more is under consideration than the birth of the Son of man, in being born of his mother without having a father, he has, needless to say, a 'rising' that is virginal. He reveals a prelude to his human begetting that is lovely beyond that of all other sons of man,* and here too, 'his name is Rising.'* In the unique distinction of his 'rising', he has never had, and never will have, an equal.

Finally, no less humble and no less wonderful than his birth from the Father before the ages and his birth from his mother in time, is the 'rising' by which he is born every day in the hearts of his faithful. The Holy Spirit bears witness that 'to those who fear the name of God, the Sun of justice' has risen up, 'with healing in his wings.'* In all these ways, then, the begetting of Christ takes place, and there is good reason to conclude: 'His name is Rising.'*

9. But what comes next in this passage: 'And where he is, there will be a rising out,'* leaves unexplained what exactly it is that is going to rise. It seems to direct us to another passage of scripture where we can find a meaning for this phrase. So we look elsewhere, and find it written that, where he was, 'righteousness will rise forth, and abundance of peace,'* and a new birth for his whole church will bud forth from his fruitful rising.

But listen very carefully: there is something profoundly mysterious about whom all this is being said to the high priest's bride. Within the church, the high priest, who is the symbol of the true Rising and of the great priest, also himself, to some extent, bears the name of 'Rising'. This may be because it is his task, like a sun perpetually rising, to irradiate the darkness of this world, or because the first and foremost place in the church ought to be allotted only by God's choice, not by human vocation or taking it upon oneself or by hereditary right or election. 'Where he is', all other priests and pontiffs ought to have a rising like his own, so that 'no one takes the honor to himself, but only the man who is called by God, as Aaron was.'*

Heb 5:4

10. But the man who wears the tiara of the supreme pontiff, acting as vicar for the great Priest who is in heaven, has not merely one crown on his head, but, as is here prophesied, he has two. He is distinguished with the honor of both royal and priestly power.* Thanks to the ministrations of those who passed from the babylonian captivity to the christian religion—in other words, the generous donation of christian princes who offer him the substances of tangible magnificence—he has the trappings of royal power, and likewise in his own priesthood, the dignity of sovereign administration.

Cf. Ez 5:2

In fact, it is not only two crowns he has upon his head, but rather every crown, of royal as well as priestly glory. God, the eternal Prince, has arranged that through his hand, and the hands of bishops under his authority, all coronations, of kings and of bishops, should be performed. But these kings are not even considered to bear the name of kings, until they receive anointing and the crown, from the pontiff's hand. If they are to rule, truly and profitably, they must submit themselves to the bride of Christ with bended knee and bowed head, as her servants. They must openly promise to be her defenders and champions, and accept the guardianship of the church's peace.

So, when kings come to the church for their coronations, it is as if they are carrying the rough and shapeless metal which has to be shaped into their crowns. In the same way, when they receive the consecrated crowns from the bishop's hand, by this very fact, they make public avowal that they hold the right to this glory and all that goes with it, solely from the generosity of Christ and the gift of his holy church. So those who presented bare metal, receive in its stead, crowns, but only on condition that these crowns should be a perpetual memorial to this in the Lord's temple.* In other words, these crowns will keep unavoidably before them the memory of their solemn promise, and that they received their crowns for a special purpose: to remove from the church heresies and schisms and never to cease vigorously attacking and harassing the church's enemies.

Cf. Zc 6:14

11. The high priest is seated, then, presenting the image of the eternal priest.* Yes, he sits, but not merely in his priestly chair, but also in the way the prophet foretold: 'he sits and rules upon his throne,'* a symbol of the majestic power that holds both the royal throne and the priestly chair of the eternal high priest. This is why he almost seems to represent two distinct roles within his own

Cf. Bernard, Ep. 244.2-3; SBOp 3:135-6.

Cf. Zc 6:13

person, and like Melchisedech, or rather, like the Lord Jesus, to be both priest and king.* *Gn 14:17*
He is like the 'new man',* who brings about a *Cf. Eph 2:15* state of peace within his one person, holding within himself the duality of kingship and priesthood.

Who is not filled with wonder to see the bride of Christ bearing rule like this over the persons of kings, humbling the haughty necks of princes, even calling kings into being, giving kings commands and becoming their rulers? Who but can marvel to see her set up in pride before all men, so that the rulers of this world do not think they possess their worldly glory, and do not dare to make any use of it, unless it comes to them from the bride's hand?

This 'joining of the bride's thighs', so very ingenious and wonderful, has for end 'peaceful understanding',* and buttresses her secur- *Cf. Zc 6:13* ity, while protecting her chastity. It has been fashioned by the hand and by the artistry of her Beseleel,* who was truly called 'the son of *Cf. Ex 35:30* the carpenter',* namely, the only Son of the *Cf. Mt 13:55* Father, her spouse.

12. But if any of these kings, whom the church has crowned, should make a tyrannous assault on this 'joining', in other words, on the church's covenant of peace, such a man would surely be guilty of ingratitude. He would be dishonoring his own mother, repaying her gift of glory with shame, receiving a crown of gold and offering a crown of thorns. They would be 'an adulterous generation',* *Cf. Mt 12:39* and a generation like this would have worthless offspring. It might even be more fitting

Mt 12:34

to call them 'a generation of vipers',* which tears to pieces their mother's womb as they leave it, only bursting out so as to burst it in fragments, only being born so as to destroy.

How sadly this mother laments nowadays over those children of her womb! If only her voice could be heard on high, weeping and crying after the convulsions long endured within her womb, and cursing the time that children like this should be born to her!* What follows? Is it not true that nearly everywhere, all the church's peace, freedom and honor has already been swallowed up by the presence of these kings? They are wholly forgetful of their declaration and of the pact into which they entered with God and his anointed one. They forget the solemn vow they performed, a vow made to the church and in the church. They are abominably guilty, perjured, ungrateful; they are apostates. The sword, with which the church invested them for her defense, they have suddenly unsheathed and sharpened, and they brandish it—I say it with deep distress—to slash and mutilate her.

We are not far from reverting to the original wickedness that the church knew in the days of the ancient despots. The only difference is that the very fact of being called 'christian', living in the shadow of the holy faith and having some sort of external piety, has prevented the actual shedding of blood. But this generation, that will endure no discipline and no correction, does not learn wisdom from what it suffers. In fact, it has the opposite effect: these frequent and painful batterings only make it harder, like an anvil under the hammer, as scripture says of Leviathan.*

Cf. Jb 41:15

13. But this is unimportant. All these things put together do not mislead or even for a moment hinder or disturb the hand of that great and supreme craftsman. On the contrary, they help him to press on more diligently in fashioning a necklace for his bride. They urge him forward and encourage him. So great is the art and power of this master craftsman, that no enemy, however strong, can have the slightest effect on him. Any malicious attempt to frustrate him, he seizes and wisely and powerfully bends it to his will and the adornment and service of his bride. For he is the spouse of the church,
our Lord Jesus Christ, who with God
the Father and the Holy Spirit,
lives and reigns, God,
for ever and ever.
Amen.

SERMON SIXTY-EIGHT

The beginning of the sixty-eighth sermon. How these words can be applied to the soul that loves God; in which they are first discussed with reference to the soul that has charge of other souls, and of the wonderfully profound 'joining' of diverse elements, while interiorly she strives to please the spouse, and exteriorly does not neglect to keep a firm hand on the things of this world. Then the same verse is applied to the soul whose every movement, whether at work or at rest, is directed solely, with complete freedom, to the love of her spouse alone.

'THE JOINING OF YOUR THIGHS is like a necklace, work of a master craftsman.'*

Sg 7:1

Ps 45:3

What are we to make of the fact that 'the fairest of the children of men'* should press especially on the ears of the daughters of Jerusalem mention of the most intimate parts of the bride's body? Why has so great a king no regard even for his own sacred dignity and reserve? But in fact, from this, and other similar passages in this song, we can rightly deduce that it is the Spirit who is speaking, and speaking of the secret mysteries of the most holy love. It admits only of a spiritual interpretation, and one that has been circum-

cised by the sword of the Spirit.* It will be
wiser, then, for the uncircumcised, and those
who are weak of heart or hearing, to depart
without delay, and to withdraw themselves.*
Otherwise, if somebody of this kind comes up
too hastily to the mountain, hoping to force
his way into the cloud where the spouse
is dwelling,* he would not be able to endure
the brightness, to which he is still unaccus-
tomed and for which he is very unfit. Staying
there in all his fleshliness, he would feel himself one of the animals 'to be stoned'.*

So he must wait patiently, if he be wise by
the breasts of the bride, he must console himself while he waits, with the nourishment of
their milk. The day will come when his understanding and other faculties will increase
and have the capacity for them, and then he
will put on the 'more perfect man'.* Then
in the consciousness of true love for the
spouse, he will learn, not only to feel no
embarrassment at what the spouse says, but
to take joy in it. For to modest ears, nothing
that he says sounds embarrassing; to sober
and honest minds, he says nothing that is
trivial or undelicate; but they provide for the
purified, what has been well tested, and for
the pure, what has been well strained; they
offer spiritual things to the spiritual,* and
sweet things to the lovers who are 'men after
his own heart'.*

2. So we shall now speak about the soul
that loves Jesus very affectionately, so far as
the very Spirit of love will himself bestow.
And first we must deal with the soul whose
happy and holy marriage with the spouse has

Eph 6:17

*Cf. Bernard,
SC 1.8, 11-12;
SBOp 1:6-8;
CF 4:5-7.*

Cf. Ex 24:16

Cf. Heb 12:20

Cf. Eph 4:27

Cf. 1 Co 2:13

Cf. 1 S 2:35

led, through their ecstatic and tender devotion, not only to the birth, like sons and
daughters, of spiritual insights and dispositions, but has pressed forward to gain souls.
Yet all this fruitfulness has never ceased to
increase within them the grace of their spouse.
Such a soul says in her heart what was said
long ago by Leah, a woman who was, at first,
regarded as an object of contempt.* Then,
by reason of the fruitfulness given her from
heaven, she wiped away the shame of having
red-rimmed eyes,* making up for her lack of
beauty by bearing many children. When she
gave birth to a male child, she said: 'Now my
husband will love me.'* And she said the same
when she had brought forth other sons: 'Now
my husband will be joined to me, for I have
borne him three sons.'*

Equally, the bride of Christ feels love
goading her on to win and deepen the favor
of her husband. More so, because the very
holiness of her love makes it a more piercing
goad, as well as giving it a sweeter flavor, a
more powerful force and a stronger hold on
her. It seems indisputable that the bride, the
guardian of the loving words of the spouse in
this wedding song, both before and after this,
is this kind of woman. She is eager to be a
wife and a delight to her spouse in both the
ways we mentioned, that is, anxious to be all
his in charity, and also to be fruitful in form-
ing souls.

At the very beginning of this song, these
words of hers resounded in her ears: 'They
made me keeper of the vineyard, but my own
vineyard I have not kept.'* These words are a

sigh, in fact, a reproach, drawn up from the deep abyss of love. She has longed, ardently and passionately, for the kiss of Jesus, her Solomon,* and now, having at last had for a moment the joy and bliss of experiencing it, she can scarcely endure to have laid on her the guardianship of the vineyard, that is, the care of souls. She accepts it, but as a burden.

Cf. Sg 1:2

Marriage, as the apostle says, is indeed an honorable state,* and to become dear to the spouse is a great privilege in the present and will be a seedbed of great glory in the future. But the man who has labored well and been a faithful servant, who has not been all agape for his own profit but has been wholly intent upon the salvation of souls and God's honor, has prepared a very high position for himself in heaven. Such a man has been a wise steward, knowing how to give food in due season,* and knowing too, when it is useful to distribute a measure* of advice or entreaty, of correction or consolation. Without any doubt, the supreme Master of the household will set him up over all his goods.* Clearly these things are great and very honorable and sublime, and they ought to encourage the bride, or powerfully console her, when she is fleeing in fear from the burden to be laid upon her to bear, or complaining unhappily under the weight of the burden already laid.

Cf. Heb 13:4

Cf. Mt 24:45
Cf. Lk 12:42

Cf. Mt 24:47

3. All the same, between the sweet savor of the delight experienced on the one hand, and the bitter proofs of anxious responsibility on the other, she knows a passion, an anguish and a weariness that only the spouse is aware of. He is, in fact, preparing, with craftsman's

skill and superb workmanship, to deck his bride with a most intricate necklace and to endow her with two kinds of fruitfulness. Quite clearly, he is fashioning her heart and mind, by means of holy and extraordinary ecstasies, into that peace 'which surpasses all understanding,'* but he also has in view the building up of souls. So he gives her at the same time, the glory of being called mother and a tenderness of disposition, as well as, last of all, a rich supply of the milk she needs to feed her children. But to construct this 'joining' is extremely difficult and laborious: what work it takes, what patience, what suffering! But for the spouse, the matter is not difficult at all. He is truly the Son of the great Carpenter,* and he has as his own all his Father's knowledge of his craft, so that with him, 'no word can be impossible', or seem difficult.*

4. It is on the bride that the full weight of this work falls, and all the difficulty. The task of fashioning this necklace of hers goes toilsomely on, upon her own back, while she stands there, bearing the pressure of the fashioning hands and receiving their blows. Has anyone the wisdom to understand this, to be able to weigh with exactitude the thought behind each blow that falls on her and what determines their force?* For, according to the apostle, the state of wedlock is a serious one, and a married woman must of necessity think of 'the things of this world, and how to please her husband,'* and this gives her a divided interest. And indeed, this marriage law of division, which the apostle mentions, also affects the Lord's bride, and

she is forced to endure very frequent and distressing constraints.

With her whole heart given to the service of God, she is afraid of becoming involved in worldly affairs, and flees away from them. But when she turns away, they follow her, when she flees, they pursue her, when she seeks seclusion, they loom over her all the more threateningly. In fact, they unearth her in her seclusion and drag her, however reluctant, from her retreat. And so the daughter of Zion is taken prisoner and marched away, as if to the court of Pilate, or rather, as if to the cross. Now she must listen to insults and terrors, the outcries of litigation, the complaints of tax collectors, the hubbub of their contradictions, the taunts of servants, the sobbing of her children. What a world away all this is from heavenly devotion, how alien to interior peace, how divorced from the joy of the Holy Spirit!* And yet, we *Cf. Rm 14:17* believe that it is by these things, as if by the craftsman's hammers, that the bride's heart is trained to brotherly love, to humility and patience. It is from such crude and lowly stuff that a precious necklace is formed for her, by the craftsman's hand of her spouse.

5. Of course, she subjects herself to this harsh and humiliating servitude for love of her spouse, and she has no other motive for this service, which is why, for the Lord's bride, 'all these things work together for her good.'* *Rm 8:28* That 'good' is the only thing for which she most ardently longs, it is the only thing to which she has any desire to cling. For her night of darkness is succeeded by a more

lovely brightness, and after the torments of worldly cares, there comes the light of a sabbath of interior peace, even more joyous than before.* From the slavery of her toil, the bride bears away what we might call adornments for her attire. She is deeply conscious that her hands labor 'at the basket',* but not in the same way as 'Israel according to the flesh',* or as those who, still today, bear this wretched servitude in the vain hope of fleshly glory. No, it is as the 'handmaid of the Lord',* as the bride of Jesus, as mother and nurse to the children of God.

But in the various actions of her sons, she contemplates their progenitor, her spouse, and it is this that enables her to serve with great patience, to lay upon her shoulder the weight of bearing humiliations, complaints, insults, murmurs. She does not hold their sins against them, but returns good for evil,* heaping lighted coals of charity on their heads,* until they are also set on fire, and with clothes that once were black, and wear an appearance all of light.

6. O, how difficult this is, or rather, how impossible, unless done by the hand of a craftsman who knows all things, by the arm of one who can do all things! See how 'the giants tremble underneath the waters,'* saying to him who set them there: 'You have placed men over our heads.'* You, perhaps, will be of the opinion that this is said by those who have submitted, for Christ's sake, to the commands of men. For my part, while not disagreeing with you, I think all the same that this is far more likely to be the voice of those

who are forced to carry the very people who, apparently, are carrying them. It is clearly about these men that scripture says: 'Their children will be carried on their shoulders, and dandled upon the knee.* These words, coming from the Holy Spirit, refer to the bride's charity, for she very patiently carries them, as if on her shoulders, and very lovingly, forgetting her injuries and remembering only her duty, her responsibility, the grace she has been given, she as it were, 'dandles them on her knee'. In fact, she goes down on her knees to intercede for their sins; on bended knees she alleviates their sufferings, lowers herself to their weakness, and conforms to their way of life as much as charity permits.

Cf. Is 66:12

7. For the 'joining of the bride's thighs' is the skilful fastening together into union, with God as craftsman, of interests that are very different and almost opposed. It means that while she is outwardly forced to labor at vanity, inwardly she strives to serve the truth. In one way, she is violently called away, against her will, and in another, she is called back again, even more violently because in accord with her will. Necessity drags her one way, and freedom draws her the other. Both ways she is a captive, but the former is to a pressing slavery, while the latter is to a most free and blessed pressure. One side, brotherly peace is preserved by the labor of busy solicitude, and the other side, it is gently enjoyed by receiving the gift of interior tranquility and the love of Jesus. There, the 'preparation of peace'* is in the affliction of her spirit,

Cf. Eph 6:15

Cf. Ac 9:31

but here it is in the anointing of the Holy Spirit.*

All this in reference to the soul who has laid upon it the care of her brother's salvation.

8. But there is also the soul, who has received from her spouse the gift of entering into that state of freedom where her sole repose, and her sole occupation, too, is to gaze on the face of Jesus, to long for his mouth, to adhere to his side, to cling to his steps, to open wide her mouth so as to draw the Spirit from his own mouth.* This is the most pure and beautiful pleasure of 'the joining of the thighs', all the deeper for being freely experienced. However, even this repose has its toil. This total devotion does not lack a forge, nor furnace and hammer for the forge. How many are quite unable to bear the penance of this repose, and are worn away far more by it than by any kind of bodily mortification. They are unwilling to endure a good so great, and they return to former and accustomed things.

*Cf. Bernard,
SC 40.3;
SBOp 2:26;
CF 7:201.*

But the bride of Jesus has been endowed with bridal dispositions. Like a most fair and chaste woman, she strives to conform to the will of her lovely spouse all her leisure and all her activity, that is, all that she does within and without, so as to bear him sons who will be in his image and likeness.* What sons, you may ask? Listen to the apostle: 'The fruits of the Spirit', he says, 'are charity, joy, peace, patience, long-suffering, kindness, goodness',* and so on. All he here mentions proceed from the bride's womb, when the spouse has made

Cf. Gn 1:26

Ga 5:22

her conceive. Moreover, the Word's bride guards herself very wisely, so that none of these fruits could be ascribed to her own industry, but all to the hand and working of the great Workman.

With such sons is the bride made fruitful by the spouse: such are the necklaces with which she is adorned. Clearly, sons are to her the same as the adornment of a necklace. She bears her sons in pain, but receives them with joy once they are brought forth, and she co-operates laboriously with her spouse, as his hands fashion her necklace. Then afterwards, it is her adornment, making her desirable to her spouse, the Son of the Father,
who with the Father and the Holy Spirit,
lives and reigns, God,
for ever and ever.
Amen.

SERMON SIXTY-NINE

The beginning of the sixty-ninth sermon. How the navel, if it has not yet been trimmed, is a symbol of lust, and if it has been trimmed, a symbol of the chastity of the church or of the soul that seeks God. The latter is called a 'rounded bowl', therefore, because only by the hand of the Holy Spirit can it be fashioned and finished, although the one in whom this is achieved must work hard and long. From this bowl alone can the word of salvation be fittingly drunk, since it is only right that the holy should dispense what is holy.*

'YOUR NAVEL IS A ROUNDED BOWL, never lacking wine.'*

The spouse presses on with praise of the bride whom he will take to himself from Israel, at the end of time. He has already admired her charity and twofold solicitude in 'the joining of her thighs', and now he graciously extolls the force of her modesty in her 'navel'. In women, the seat of lust is in the navel, as saint Gregory confirms* on the authority of the words spoken to Job by the Lord: 'His strength is in his loins, and his power in the navel of his belly.'* This is why, in the gospel, men are ordered to have their loins girt,* obviously to indicate care for their chastity. Then, in Ezekiel, when the spouse

86

addresses the synagogue, the image of a woman, he says, 'On the day of your birth, your navel string was not cut,'* in other words, reproaching her with the stain of her inborn concupiscence. She has proudly lifted herself up against God, relying on her justice, and he is casting her down by a reminder of the shame of her filthy and degrading birth. But now, on the contrary, she is humbled, and her humiliation has reconciled her again to her spouse, and so he speaks words of consolation, or rather, words very loving and full of praise: 'Your navel is a rounded bowl, never lacking wine.'*

Ez 16:4

Sg 7:2

2. The 'navel' of our original sin, before it is cut and trimmed by the Holy Spirit, is a bowl of deadly poison, and it always 'lacks wine', though at the same time never failing to overflow for what it always has ready is water that brings death, to make every soul drunk. It is full of a muddy and slimy water. This is the reason for the spouse's rebuke to his bride, when she was burning with thirst for this kind of water: 'What do gain by going to Assyria to drink the water of its river? And what do you gain by going to Egypt to drink its muddy water?'* Without a doubt, those waters thicken with muddy slime of their impurity the joy of a good conscience; theirs is a bloody draught, and it entails death. For the waters of Egypt were changed into blood, when God struck them, and whoever drank from them, died the death.*

Jr 2:18

Cf. Ex 7:20

But now when the bride is at long last really to be freed from Egypt and to be reconciled, by an unshakeable bond of love, to her former husband, there comes very fittingly form his lips these words of praise: 'Your navel is a rounded bowl, never lacking wine.'* It is as if he were to say to her, in different words: In the past, you used to rely on the strength of the law, and it did not cut off the tinder of your concupiscence, but rather inflamed and increased it. But now, the grace of the gospel has made you so healthy, that the seat of lust has beomce the throne of modesty, and the bowl of death is a continual source of the wine of life.

3. But this is not all: the grace is not only for you, but for the whole world! In the past, it was through you that the truth of salvation, which is Christ, was proclaimed to the nations; it is likewise through you, before the second coming of the Saviour, that the world awaits the renewal of that same salvation. So it is you who are the 'rounded bowl', receiving and containing and furnishing the legality of eternal salvation. Through you, the salvation of the world came to the nations, through you the offering of the nations is to be poured back as a gift to God. This is what the apostle speaks of when he says: 'So that the offering of the nations may be acceptable, sanctified in the Holy Spirit.'* And Isaiah, too: 'They shall bring', he says, obviously meaning the sons of Israel, 'all your brethren from all the nations, as an offering to the Lord . . . . to my holy mountain, my Israel, says the Lord, just as the sons of Israel bring their offerings in a clean vessel to the house of the Lord.'*

Just think what the size of this bowl must

be, able to receive so great an offering! Think of its great roundness, or perfection, since it was rounded on the lathe by the hand of Solomon the Great! Think how holy it is, how pure, since it is through and in it that 'the offering of the nations' is said to be 'acceptable and sanctified in the Holy Spirit.'* No wonder it is described as 'never lacking wine', since in the present life it provides us with grace, and in the life to come, it will serve us with glory. Indeed, they 'never lack wine', those who are not contented merely with their own salvation and keep nothing back from Jesus for their own personal use. They generously share out, for the good of all, the grace they have been freely given, and so 'they never lack', because they are always overflowing to others.

Rm 15:16

Avarice, on the other hand, is always in want, but the riches of generosity are inexhaustible. The fruit of generosity becomes a blessing,* and when the hand of Jesus is raised in blessing, the reaper will fill his own hand, however meager the seed be sowed. But I should not say: will fill, and make it future, since there is no question of waiting for the increase. The blessing takes effect at once, and 'he who sows in blessings', immediately 'he will reap in blessings.'* And it is quite clear that when the apostle says: he will reap, he intends it to mean that he will not cease to reap. For God, the richest of rewarders, says: 'Today I declare that I will return to you double.'* The most kindly of spouses, too, now makes this splendid statement to his bride, that this bowl should never

Cf. Ps 37:26

2 Co 9:6

Zc 9:12

lack wine, or, to put it better, it will always draw richly from his richness, bubbling over with the richness of his kindness, flowing out to everybody, overflowing within himself.

4. And notice how the spouse is at the same time both prudent and chaste in this description of his bride. In praising her navel, that is, her modesty, he expressly mentions 'wine', so as to make it clear that no one is worthy of the office of preaching the gospel if he has been scorched by any evil brand of wantonness. In fact, 'he must be well thought of by outsiders.'* This is especially so for those who have necessarily to deal with outsiders in the work of general salvation, in order that, as the apostle says, the Word of God may speed on without check,* and be glorified. Hence these words of Isaiah: 'You shall be called holy to the Lord, the servants of our God.'*

5. The first thing he says is 'holy', and the second is 'servants', because, as the apostle says, 'the mystery of faith' ought to be held in 'a pure conscience.'* It ought to be like the heavenly manna, in a golden tabernacle,* something most holy and not to be handled or served except by holy men. This is why it most expressly says, 'You shall be called holy', and not, 'you will be holy,' requiring in God's servants even the perfume of a holy reputation.

How wearying to live in these evil days! How shameful is our modern shamelessness! To our grief, wherever we turn our eyes, we behold the most pure word of God distributed in vessels of the most glaring impurity, and the very mysteries of the sacred altar, in all their awesomeness, are being taken and handed out as if they were no more than ordinary food. Yet, in whatever relates to the office of preaching, the Lord has made their tongue cleave to the roof of their mouth.* *Cf. Ez 3:26* For their navel string has not been cut, and their navel is not like 'a rounded bowl', so that it always lacks wine. Yes, it lacks the wine of life, which it is damnation not to possess, but it never goes without the cups of death, with which it is sadly well supplied and for which it miserably thirsts.

6. Consequently, and this is something to be specially observed, both in this and the previous verse, the spouse goes out of his way, in praising his beloved, to mention grace. In the verse before, what he praised in 'the joining of the thighs' was the craftsman's hand, and here, in the navel, which he compares to a 'rounded bowl', he has assigned to the Holy Spirit, the duty of acting as turner, to make the bowl round on his lathe. Why should he do this, unless he is anxious to impress upon his loved one the memory of grace? He wants to make it quite plain to his beloved that if even for one moment, she neglected to remember grace, she would rightly be no longer worthy of receiving that grace.

So these words of the spouse, as we have said, are addressed to the Shulamite,* namely, *Cf. 1 K 1:3* the church of the Israelites, which is to be reconciled to Christ at the end of time. It is her future hope to equal the grace of the apostles and to be like the early church, a

Cf. Lk 24:47

chosen arrow that the Lord can direct in order to save all nations.* But in the meantime, the church of the gentiles, married to Christ her spouse by an inviolable bond, is anxious to cut off the wanton string of her navel, following the law of chastity she has been given, and since she cannot at all attempt this through her own strength or endeavor, she surrenders to the grace of her spouse, as if to be turned on the lathe by the hand of the heavenly craftsman.

This is the cause of that loving cry to her helper for chastity that we find in the psalm:

Ps 26:2

'Cleanse my heart and my mind.'* And again: 'Lord, Lord, the strength of my salvation, do not give me up to the desire of the

Ps 140:7,8

wicked.'* With a craftsman, and the most dexterous craftsman of all is the Wisdom of God, it is necessary, part of the day's work like turning on a lathe, 'suddenly to enrich

Sir 11:21

the poor man,'* as the Wiseman puts it. From the rough and nobbly wood, he suddenly forms a rounded bowl, one that will clearly never lack wine, but from the rich overflow of its heart, bubble over with offerings of praise to its maker.

7. So then, the bride's navel is a rounded bowl in the hand of her spouse, from which, while this life lasts, he drinks whatever fruit of the vine his bride has been able to prepare for him in the days of her earthly pilgrimage. And afterwards, on the day of solemn festival and rejoicing, he will drink from it, with even greater gladness, the vintage of another genera-

Cf. Lk 22:18

tion, which will then fill the bowl.* O never-failing fullness of this bowl, who is worthy to think of you, who may lovingly hold you in the life to come? Who may thirst enough for you in this present life? At the present day, that bowl, by the spouse's generosity, is not without wine to refresh any thirst of his, but on the last day, it will be enriched with an overflowing fulness, so as wholly to inebriate him. Then, as it says in later verses of this song, the bride will give him 'spiced wine to drink, the juice of my pomegranates.'*   *Sg 8:2*

So the bride's navel, that is, the church's chastity, awaits from God an eternity of praise, because from this very chastity, as from a pure and costly bowl, she will eternally give her Creator the drink of praise and thanksgiving. For those words, 'never lacking wine',* signify, as we have pointed out, an   *Sg 7:2* eternal and neverfailing fulness.

8. Moreover, any holy soul, who by the gift of the Spirit of love, has been given the privilege and title of bride, can rightly claim these admiring words as her own. Of course, she must cut off her navel string, or round out her bowl, so that it is fit for the spouse to drink from. In plain words, she must circumcise her concupiscence and completely renew her chastity, and in doing this, she must necessarily take great pains. How much she takes depends on how much she is possessed by a deep longing for this holy beauty and moved by the influence of the Spirit of love. So it is a continual and tireless need for her, this cutting of the navel string and rounding of the bowl, and although she resists with all vigor the onslaughts of

concupiscence, and applies herself to healing her weakness, all the same, as long as she struggles on,* the end of the contest hangs in the balance. While still among the risks of the fighting, it would be rash indeed to rejoice too quickly.

Here on this earth, the only safety is to be ever doubtful of her own weakness, and never to stop drinking the wine of compunction from her bowl, which is not yet fully rounded. It is to grieve with the apostle and exclaim: 'Unhappy man that I am, who will free me from the body of this death?'* And to say with David, also: 'I am utterly wretched and prostrate, I go mourning all the day long, for my loins are filled with burning.'* Believe me, to grieve so anxiously for these reasons, is to gird up the loins or cut the navel string, and to form a rounded bowl for the service of the spouse.

9. And it is from this bowl that, while life lasts, the spouse drinks the 'old wine', the wine of compunction. It is with this wine, arising from the very humiliation of her sorrow, that the bride gives joy to her spouse's heart.* But in the future, when the scar of cutting off the navel string has completely gone, he will drink new wine, in his Father's kingdom, from the same bowl, and the bride will drink with him.* And so that bowl, as the spouse says, 'never lacks wine',* because in this life, it always offers what this life needs, and in that blessed life, it offers what that blessedness deserves, to the praise and glory of her spouse, the only Son of the Father, who with the Father and the

Holy Spirit, lives and reigns,
God, for ever and ever.
Amen.

SERMON SEVENTY

The beginning of the seventieth sermon. How
these words are specially applicable to the holy
mother of the Lord, whose blessed childbearing
is symbolized by the 'belly', just as her virginal
chastity was by the 'navel', which was praised
in the previous sermon. How the surrounding
lilies point to the guardianship of the angels, or
the protection of the Holy Spirit, inspiring her
with the thought of chastity. Or else, it may
indicate the chaste thoughts and dispositions
that surround her, or the company of holy
souls who imitate her chastity and trust in her
protection.

'YOUR BELLY IS LIKE a heap of
wheat, encompassed with lilies.'*
Amid all the ranks of the saints, the
first place for humility, purity and tender love
is held by the blessed virgin, the mother of
Jesus, and in the same way, she shines out
gloriously, above all God's lovers, for the
greatness of her charity. This is why that
title of unique glory, which the Spirit of
charity, in his gracious goodness, makes common to all souls that love Jesus, has been
bestowed by him with special reason on the
one who loves him very much more: the
title of 'bride of God', and she is called God's
bride and is his bride.* It is she who is truly

Sg 7:2

Cf. Sg 4:8

'the mother of fair love',* as the church sings
of her;* she is the teacher of knowledge† of
it, the craftsman who trains us in it,** its
lawgiver, the go-between who brings about
love's covenant with us.

Obviously, 'happy is the man who watches
daily at her gates and waits at her doorposts.'*
At last, after long waiting, he is finally
admitted to the heart of her holy marriage
chamber, where he may be privileged to
understand something of the perfume of the
charity of Christ, overflowing there in its
scented abundance. It will be for him 'the
life-giving fragrance of life itself.'*

Everything, then, in this marriage song, is
directed principally to Mary, the principal
bride of Jesus. This remains true, whatever
form the words take, whether from the lips of
the spouse to the bride or, in her turn, of the
bride to the spouse, or from something she
may say when training the maidens, or from
their wonder and questioning, as these daughters of Jerusalem ponder over her words.

2. In fact, in her own self, Mary the bride
is the highest and most distinguished model
of love, and from her overflowing fullness,
each of the maidens receives as much as her
capacity allows.* Since she is 'full of grace',†
it perpetually abounds within her, a never-
failing source of marvelous pleasure as well as
total richness to every spirit, angelic and
human. This is why the woman who saves
not only men but even those who work like
beasts of burden,* does not consider it
robbery to adapt that tender saying of the
Word of God: 'If anyone thirst, let him come

Sir 24:24

**Chapter at Cister-
cian Vespers for
Nativity B.V.M.
†Cf. Ws 8:4
**Cf. Ws 8:6.*

Pr 8:24

2 Co 2:16

**Cf. Eph 4:7
†Cf. Lk 1:28*

Ps 36:6

Jn 7:37

Sir 24:26

to me and drink.'* And that other saying, too: 'Come to me, all who desire me, and eat your fill of my produce.'* So any soul who longs for a holy love for the Word, should listen to her wise invitation. He should make haste, he should go to her, he should come close, he should cling. Believe me—or better still, believe the Holy Spirit: to gain the love of Jesus there is no shorter way than to contemplate the beauty of this unique, incomparable and immense charity.

3. The Holy Spirit, therefore, makes it clear that whatever is repeatedly said in her special praise, she can claim, almost as if by right, though I must confess I am unworthy of explaining this as it deserves. For this reason, I have up to now, laid a finger to my lips, not wanting to struggle in my clumsy fashion with a matter so great and so unfitted to my strength. Instead of soaring into a eulogy of the bride, I might only reveal my own presumption. So I forebore, leaving this task to those stronger than myself, preferring to be silent than to speak unworthily of one who deserves to be described by the tongue of angels rather than of men.

Yet, when I think it over, when Jesus was speaking to the crowds, it was not one of the band of the apostles, not one of the council of the elders, but simply one of the women there in the crowd who 'lifted up her voice', and proclaimed that the womb that bore him was blessed.* The example of this woman has given me the courage to dare, in my turn, to say something about the blessedness of this womb. And in sober truth, above all that can

Lk 11:27

be said or thought, that womb is blessed indeed, pregnant with so sacred an offspring, heavy with so light a burden, guardian of a trust so precious. That womb is a marriage chamber of very great tenderness, rich in the most noble seed, and it contains a great and holy secret. It has knowledge of great mystery and it bears very great dignity.

4. But clearly, that womb was blessed even before it carried the Lord. Day and night, with a most pure desire and the longing of a holy and consecrated love, it prepared itself to bear its holy burden. In the silence of her heart, Mary said to herself: 'Let him kiss me with the kiss of his mouth.'* *Sg 1:1* There has never been another soul, or rather, there has never been one of the blessed spirits, not even from that most blissful of the nine choirs that takes its name from the fire of charity and refreshes the heat of its immense love by the continual contemplation of eternity and the ceaseless praise of the holy Trinity: no, not even among the cherubim has any one made progress like hers in desiring and receiving this kiss.

So then, to make her ready for such great grace, from her mother's womb she was fashioned* by him who 'establishes the *Cf. Ps 139:13* heavens',* and every single moment, during *Cf. Jb 28:27* the successive stages by which God 'established' her, the fullness of grace was built up. One day she would become God's mother, and then an angel would call her 'full of grace'.* So her womb is blessed in the very *Lk 1:28* manner of its establishment in blessedness, yet it is far more blessed when it finally, in a divine and indescribable way, receives its most blessed burden. Blessed indeed, though, most blessed, is that womb when it bore him, when it formed him, when it was in labor with him, when it brought him to birth.

5. That womb gave birth to Jesus, but it was not thereafter deprived of any part of its blessedness. When Jesus left his mother's body, in which he had been cherished and nourished, he left a blessing behind him. He sanctified her womb when he entered it, he filled it when he dwelt within it, and then, when he bade it farewell, he consecrated it and strengthened it with his full blessing. That blessing overflowed on outward things, but without losing its first grace which it continually poured into her. Jesus came forth from his mother so as to bless her virginal eyes also, by showing her his face. He came forth to sanctify her mouth by the beautiful kiss of his own mouth,* to make blessed her breasts by pressing his lips to them, to consecrate her hands, her lap, her knees, every part of her, by the infinite sweetness of his sacred body as she held him to her.

So, 'all the glory of the king's daughter is from within.'* It came from within, but no part of that glory went to waste within or retreated from within. Every single one of the gifts of God's mother, whether interior or exterior, are signs of salvation. Grace was added to grace, glory was heaped on glory, and as her crowning virtue grew, nothing went to waste, not even the least touch of her humility. Although 'full of grace', she could always be enriched by a new increase of

Sg 1:1

Ps 45:13

fullness, but however this increase overflowed, no suggestion of vanity had power to spoil its bloom, not for an instant. God 'looked on' the purity of his mother, just as he had 'looked on the humility of his handmaid.'*   *Lk 1:48*

Yes, God 'looked on' her, and while he looked, he enriched her and strengthened her and rewarded her. He looked indeed, and saw that, just as this most blessed of mothers kept her virginity intact despite the glory of her fruitfulness, so did her humility remain intact and indestructible, though she had reached the heights of perfection. And it was in this way, as we have said above, that most blessed womb poured out its blessedness far and wide. There was no question of careless waste, but only of revealing the Sun of justice to those who fear God; in this way, His fervor glowed for him above all others, and took its brightness from him, greater brightness than anyone else received.

In short, just as all grace and glory flowed from this woman's body, so it can be said that every generation of saints truly arose from her by what we can only call the wonderful mystery of divine fruitfulness. Let me repeat it: the mother of Jesus is not only the mother of our glorious head, Jesus Christ, mediator between God and man, but she is also the mother of all who love Jesus, of the whole of Jesus' sacred body.*   *Cf. 1 Co 6:15* In fact, if Eve is said to be the mother of all the living,*   *Cf. Gn 3:20* though she brought us all forth to death and became mother of wrath for all who would one day arise from her, how much more truly can we call Mary the mother of the living?

She brought life to all generations of the
faithful, and became for them the mother
of grace.

6. There is something very fitting, then,
in what is said to her by the spouse, who is,
of course, the son of her womb. He says to
her: 'Your belly is like a heap of wheat.'*
One grain of wheat fell from heaven, and
from it has grown a huge heap of wheat, as
the number of the faithful multiplies. O, how
pre-eminent is the fruitfulness of this glorious
virgin! How incomparably exalted is the glory
of holy church, who can claim for herself a
family of such nobility and glory in the high
descent of so great a brother and so great a
mother! So 'belly', which is compared by the
Holy Spirit to a heap of wheat, is a very apt
symbol of the holy fruitfulness that was
enriched with a divine offspring, just as
'navel', which was likened to a 'rounded
bowl',* symbolizes the celibacy of virginal
holiness, in which the cup of eternal salvation
was to be offered to all people. This bowl is
never for a moment without the draughts of
this heavenly wine, and it will be so eternally.
Ever full and overflowing, it invites all who
thirst,* seeking and thirsting only for the
thirsty. Here on earth, this bowl offers us
holiness and grace, and in heaven it gives us
the drink of life and glory.

After this praise of the navel, that is, of
chastity, we come naturally to the commendation of the curving belly, that is, to the rich
offspring of fertility. There is a clear sequence
of thought by which the virginal fruitfulness
and the fruitful virginity of the virgin-mother

mutually adorn each other.* All the same, the fruitfulness of God's mother must not be judged solely by the actual conception of the Son of man. According to belief of the Catholic faith, this glorious mother conceived God first in her heart rather than in her flesh,* and this conception was far more fruitful. And so, according to this way of looking at it, her belly has every right to be likened to 'a heap of wheat', because the divine conception of the Word of God in her virginal heart contained the mystery of great and indescribable fruitfulness. To conceive virtues fruitfully is truly 'a heap of wheat', for it is a great pile of merits and a mass of graces. Clearly and unmistakably blessed is 'the fruit of this womb',* because, at the blessing of the Lord himself, when it gave birth to the only Son of the Father, with him was born a crop of every virtue, the fulness of every grace.

7. But this most blessed belly is 'encompassed with lilies',* because before giving birth and while giving birth and after giving birth, she was enclosed on every side by the surrounding wall of spotless virginity, and so we sing of her in the office.* That embankment of lilies is tender and gentle, yet nothing is more terrible to the enemy, nothing more impenetrable to evil spirits. He who 'feeds among the lilies'* rests here tranquilly, for the 'heap of wheat' is there for him to feed on, and the encompassing lilies are at hand to give him shade, to refresh him with the breath of their perfume, to stir him on to love. 'Until the day breathes and the shadows flee,'*

*Cf. Bernard, V Nat 3.9; SBOp 4:218.

*Cf. Bernard, p Epi 2: SBOp 4.315 & Guerric, Ann 2; PL 185: 121D; CF 32:42.

Lk 1:42

Sg 7:2

Vespers of B.V.M.

Sg 6:3

Sg 2:16

these lilies will not wither nor ever cease to flower. O, how sweet-scented are the lilies of chastity, how gracious, how glorious, how countless! In every tribe and nation they have come to bud, springing from this one most fruitful lily. Only he 'who counts the number of the stars'* could possibly count the number or estimate the grace of these lilies, which stand like a crown around the sacred womb of the blessed virgin.

And they do indeed encompass her, very stoutly, so that no one can possibly doubt, amid the witness of so many virgins, that Mary is the virgin of virgins, even though a mother. They encompass her, in case any uncircumcised and unclean person, in the presence of so many claims for modesty, should in some way have any way of disguising his own immodesty. Yes, that belly is encompassed with lilies, so that whoever approaches it, is attracted by their lovely whiteness, affected by their scent, and puts on the same disposition of holiness and sweetness.

But not only virginal chastity is a lily. The chaste bed of holy matrimony also has its lilies, all the more wonderful in their bloom as they struggle to persevere amid the thorns that spring up on every side. The Holy Spirit protects them, and though there are so many sharp points to prick them, they are not seriously wounded. And widowed continence has its lilies too, eager in its practice of holy virginity. It is like a lily curving upwards, and what it lacks in physical virginity, it strives to repair by an increase of humility and religion. And finally, there are lilies, in a penitential

Ps 147:4

chastity, which can be applied like medicine to inflamed members to restore their former wholesomeness.

8. All these lilies converge into a single encircling crown, they all join in one 'odor of sweetness',* so that among themselves and within themselves, they may feed the virgin's Son, he who is uniquely the lily.* But they encompass, surround and crown her from whom this same lily has marvelously sprung. Whatever share they have in her virtue, they restore to her as if by mutual homage, bending down to adore her like drooping lilies. Whatever in them is gleamingly pure and sweet-scented, they safeguard by her help and protect by calling upon her name. So, for this belly to be encompassed by these lilies means that it encompasses the lilies themselves, and when it is crowned by the glorious circle they form around it, this really means it has given them a crown of glory.

9. But also, these lilies come from 'a rich field which the Lord has blessed,'* and the beauty of this field, the psalmist tells us, is the Lord's.* No, if these lilies are to be covered in glorious garments and 'labor not nor spin,'* this can only be if they encompass this sacred belly with humble, tender devotion and reverence. In fact, they have encompassed it with sleepless care, from the very womb of her mother, treating it as the bridal chamber of the spouse and the home of Wisdom. This lily has grown among thorns,* and they have watched in case the spine of any thorn—I do not say, should prick her—but should even touch her in passing. It is not she

Cf. Phil 4:18

Cf. Sg 2:1

Gn 27:27

Cf. Ps 50:11

Mt 6:28

Cf. Sg 2:2

had any need of this protecting border of
lilies, but they owed her this service by right,
and to pay it was beneficial to them and to
their lady.

Cf. Lk 1:35

Soon the Holy Spirit overshadowed her,*
and the Wisdom of God, instantly present,

Cf. Pr 9:1

built a house for himself with all his might.*
Then, like a lily taking its origin from the

Cf. Jn 1:13

field of heaven,* God inspired her to seal an
immediate treaty with virginity. That she

Cf. Pr 31:25

might be clothed with strength and beauty,*
this first of all women 'set her hand to mighty

Pr 31:19

things, and her fingers seized the spindle.'* In
this task of busying her fingers at the spindle,
think what fresh and infinitely delicate
thoughts were set to work, what wise plans,
what consecrated dispositions. For wool and
flax, the raw materials of this work, were
replaced by a determined humility and an
unshakable vow to protect her virginity.

'Blessed', therefore, 'is the womb that bore

Lk 11:27

you,'* Lord Jesus! Once you encompassed it
with holy lilies, with the trusty guardianship
of a border of holy angels. You spread around
it the sacred longings and attitudes of a
heavenly intention; you bound around it the
rampart of your protection and inspiration.
Now, in heaven, you have crowned it with the
glory of all your saints, to the honor and glory
of your name, who, with the Father and the
Holy Spirit, live and reign, God,
for ever and ever.
Amen.

SERMON SEVENTY-ONE

The beginning of the seventy-first sermon.
That the belly of the bride, that is, of the
church or of the soul who loves God, is to
meditate devoutly on God's law, and the fruit
of this is the spiritual encouragement of our
neighbor and a renewal in divine love.

'YOUR BELLY IS LIKE a heap of
wheat, encompassed with lilies.'*   *Sg 7:2*
Scripture tells us that Jesus was
speaking to the crowds, and one of the
women who was there, filled with wonder at
the power of his words, broke forth into this
cry of praise.* Not content merely to praise   *Lk 11:27*
Jesus alone, she went on to celebrate the
womb that was burdened with so great a
pledge and the breasts that were favored with
so sacred a nursling. Jesus, who alone deserves
to be praised and glorified, accepted the
admiring exclamation of this woman. I do
not know whether it was more out of
humility or kindness. It was characteristic of
his humility that what she claimed solely for
his mother, he himself made clear was not
applicable to her alone. It was a mark of his
true mother, but he denied that it belonged to
no one else. On the other hand, it was
characteristic of his kindness that he trans-
ferred that unique grace of being 'blessed' to

a universal basis, and poured the glory of his mother's fruitfulness into the lap of the whole church, as a grace for everyone. For his answer was: 'No, rather call blessed those who hear the Word of God and keep it.'*

2. So, with the approval of Jesus, the praise that was meant for one, is distributed to all, in so far as he interprets his mother and his nurse as being the whole church. She hears and keeps the Word of God, and so he is carried in her womb and suckled at her breasts. Now, since he who speaks in the gospel and he who speaks in the Song is the same spouse and has the identical theme of praise, namely, the bride's belly, it must be clear to everybody, without detriment to the praise that is due to the virgin mother.

Moreover, to take up again the story of the Shulamite, that is, the church that at the end of time will be taken from Israel to be married to Christ,* it is only right that the praise of the navel should be followed by a commendation of the belly. For the navel, as we have explained, symbolizes the chastity of those who go all round the world to preach Christ's name, and the belly stands for the fruitfulness of their teaching and the usefulness of what they preach. This is why this belly is fittingly compared to a heap of wheat, because those who have been ordered by the Father of the household to hand out the wheat in due measure,* must certainly have a great heap of this kind themselves. This house is a true 'house of bread'; obviously the place where Christ was born has a right to be called 'Bethlehem'.* He who 'feeds among the lilies',* can feed among them very easily in the place of his birth.

    3. Yes, the bride's belly is truly 'like a heap of wheat, encompassed with lilies.'* Blessed is the servant who will take care to collect this wheat by attending to his spiritual reading and being devoted to his meditations.* Then the bride can feast on the book of holy law, which the Lord her God has given her, and it can fill her stomach.* Otherwise, how could she lift up her head when her beloved comes to her from a journey, and she has nothing to set before him?* It will be very distressing, in fact, it will be quite scandalous, to choose then to go begging when it is rather the time for generous giving that has come. At that hour, she will not have time to disturb the sleep of a sleeping friend with importunate pleas to borrow; she will not be able to arouse him, when his door is shut and his children are with him in bed.* Rather, she will be on the watch for herself and for the household over which she has been set, in case it should be disappointed when the time comes for food.* And as well as this, she will be on the watch for the unexpected guest on his journey so as not to incur the great shame and disgrace of having sent him away hungry.*

    'Do your best', says the apostle to Timothy, 'to present yourself to God as one approved, a workman who has no need to be ashamed, rightly handling the word of truth.'* You will 'present yourself as a workman who need not be ashamed', if you have the word of encouragement always ready, and if the living

Sg 2:16

Sg 7:2

Cf. Gregory the Great, Hom. in Ezech. *I,x,11; PL 76:890B.*

Cf. Ezk 3:3

Cf. Lk 11:6

Cf. Lk 11:7

Cf. Lk 12:37

Cf. Lk 11:10

2 Tim 2:15

reply of good works comes in answer to the word of teaching. Yes, you have escaped the danger of incurring twofold shame if you have used this 'heap of wheat' both to provide all you need for your own livelihood and to enable you to run with ready and resolute charity to help your needy brothers. You cannot be put to shame, if you are coming with your loaves to succor the friend who flees to you when confronted with grave danger, if you break bread for your little ones when they ask it, or press it upon them when they do not ask.* In short, you cannot be put to shame if you supply bread for all the household, while at the same time not depriving your own self of the nourishment of your bread.

Is there not unbearable shame in these words: 'Physician, heal yourself!',* and in these: 'What right have you to recite my commandments?',* and: 'You who teach others, will you not teach yourself?'* So, when your household sits down to a meal, if you are wise, you will first sit down yourself, and then you will be able to serve them easily and happily. In your charity to your neighbor, remember that your nearest neighbor is yourself, Or, at least, be like the servants who wait at table and do not remain fasting; when everyone has had his fill, join company with the Canaanite women and her whelps and eat some of the scraps which remain.*

4. 'From the fruit of a man's mouth', says Solomon, 'his belly will be filled, and the yield of his lips will satisfy him.'* The 'fruit

Cf. Lm 4:4

Lk 4:23

Ps 50:16
Rm 2:21

Cf. Mt 15:27

Pr 18:20

of a man's mouth' is what he preaches, words
that are usefully distributed to give glory
to God and encouragement to our brothers.
But it is to be a real 'man' who preaches, not
someone who is more of a woman, women
having been forbidden by the apostle to speak
in church.* Those who live in a womanish   *Cf. 1 Co 14:34*
fashion destroy by their example whatever
they have erected by their words. No, if
someone is a man, he will not only speak like
a man, he will act like one. 'From the fruit of
his mouth he will fill his belly', 'and the yield
of his lips will satisfy him.'* Since he is gain-   *Pr 18:20*
ing the salvation of others by his preaching,
and conforming his own life to what he
preaches, both from them and from himself
he is reaping great personal fruit.

Solomon himself says the same: 'Apply
your heart to knowledge, my son, and it will
be a delight to you, if you keep it within your
belly and have it ready on your lips.'* Kept   *Pr 22:17,18*
in the belly, it comes sweetly and profitably
to the lips. Only then, when 'from the
abundance of the heart, the mouth speaks,'*   *Mt 12:34*
is the word profitable on the lips. So 'the
belly' of the bride is the guardian of God's
word. In a belly like this, food is brought
together in safety and digested with power
and then advantageously assimilated into the
body to bring health to all the members,
limbs and senses.

5. 'Blessed is that belly, and blessed is
its fruit',* for the 'heap of wheat' which is in   *Cf. Lk 1:42*
it, or rather, which it is, never ceases to
furnish the bread of eternal life. Moreover,

'streams of living water' are always flowing from it.* The Lord Jesus chose a belly of this nature as a suitable place for his birth and formation, for it was one where he would never suffer from hunger or thirst. And now, if we look, he is preparing just such a belly in the Shulamite, for, imitating the blessed virgin-mother, she is to be both a mother to him and a bride. In fact, the man 'whose name is Origin',* is about to seek again his original cradle. He is about to return again to Bethlehem, to 'the heap of wheat',* or, as Ezekiel has it, 'to the heap of fresh fruits',* which still exist in the midst of Babylon, by the banks of the river Chobar. And it is from there, to our wonder and admiration, that the prince of Judah, and all Judah, with him, will be both able and eager to enter once more into his mother's womb and be born again.*

Who can worthily unfold the great joy of this marvel, the happiness of this conception, the solemn festival of this birth? But this rejoicing in every tribe and family will belong as much to the race of gentiles as to the sons of Israel; they will all rejoice: 'A child is born for us and a son is given to us.'* And it will be said to Judah, who at the present time is a 'hissing and a byword' to all people,* I repeat, it will be said to Judah, 'Blessed are you among women, and blessed is the fruit of your womb,'* and she will be blessed by every nation. Juda will have this 'said to her': 'because you were forsaken and held in scorn, look, you have been made majestic for ever.'* As in the days of old, 'you shall raise up the

foundation of many generations.'* The glory *Is 58:12*
of your new marriage will make you forget all
the shame of your widowhood, and in the
innumerable fruit of your teeming womb,
you will no longer remember your failure to
bear children. The Lord your God will multiply your nation, and he will do more: he
will magnify your happiness,* blessing you *Lk 1:46*
ever more abundantly than in the days of old,
when 'the Lord sent his word against Jacob
and it fell upon Israel.'* *Is 9:3*

On that day, then, you will have 'a belly
like a heap of wheat',* supplying you with all *Sg 7:2*
you could possibly need for eating and sowing, for selling and bequeathing to your
children. 'The Lord has sworn by his right
hand and by his mighty arm: 'I will not again
give your grain to be food for your enemies
. . . but those who garner it shall eat it, and
praise the Lord.'* So, by the Lord's gracious *Is 62: 8,9*
gift, it will first overflow for you to eat it, so
that the belly of your own conscience will be
filled. Then it will be for sowing, so that from
the abundance of your heart, it will pour
over onto your lips.* It will be yours to *Cf. Mt 12:34*
bequeath, so that you have it there at hand
to support the household entrusted to you.* *Cf. Lk 12:42*
Finally, it will be for selling, so that it will be
at hand for you to distribute it to the whole
realm by preaching; it will be like the coin of
the realm, namely, for the price of God's
blessing. For, says Solomon, 'The man who
holds back grain is cursed by the people, but
the blessing of the Lord is on the head of
those who sell.'* And so, by the blessing *Pr 11:26*
of God, a blessing will come to you from

Cf. Sir 44:25

Cf. Gn 12:3

every nation,* because all the peoples of the earth will be blessed when you open your mouth.*

Therefore this heap of wheat will not have round it the hedge of envy or be fenced in with the rampart of greed, so that you announce the truth of Christ grudgingly or hide it away out of envy. No, it is only encompassed with the lilies of goodness and innocence. The beauty of this lovely palisade and its sweet fragrance repells no one from participating in this wheat but rather attracts them all. Nobody will find fault with Peter for going to an uncircumcised people,* but on the contrary, the wall of partition broken down and the barrier removed,* both will come together into one house. There will no longer be a distinction between Jew and Greek.* Each will open to the other like an unfolding lily, opening out and spreading wide. Juda will not be jealous of Ephraim, Ephraim will not be jealous of Juda,* but each of them will be to the other 'the scent of life leading to life,'* and each 'will say to its neighbor: be consoled.'*

6. You too, holy soul, who by reason of your outstanding charity have won the name of 'bride' or aspire to it with great longing, if you too would receive a blessing and become 'blessed among women, and blessed the fruit of your womb',* then you must imitate the mother of the Lord. You must gather wheat into your belly, you must keep it carefully, gathering up into your heart what you have heard about Jesus.* If wisdom had been your desire, and wisdom is other than Jesus, the

spouse, then follow the advice of the Wise man: keep the commandments and the Lord will give it to you.* 'I have longed for your salvation, Lord,' he says, 'and my thoughts dwell on your law.'* Longing for Jesus, who is the true salvation of God, obviously makes it sweet and wholesome to dwell in thought on the divine law. On the other hand, if there is no desire for him, this meditation will be dry, not only useless but actually harmful. 'He who only goes in search of words,' says Solomon, 'will have nothing. But he who possesses his heart, loves his soul and keeps understanding, he will find good things.'*

What will be the good of stowing wheat away in a barn or in a chest,* if you deprive your own belly and your household of bread to eat? What good does it do to see and know great riches if there is no chance to enjoy them? Consequently, 'whoever knows what is right to do and does not do it, for him there is sin.'* Just as for the Jew, so equally for the Christian, if he makes his boast of the law:* where the Spirit does not give life, the written code kills.* If charity is not there to build, knowledge alone can only 'puff up'.* So the bride's belly is a safe place to store this wheat, since, desiring the salvation of God with all the strength of her soul, she never ceases from meditation on God's law,* which is charity.† For where her treasure is, there is her heart.* There she effectually digests, with what we could call the invisible fire of love, all the words of Jesus and whatever she has anywhere seen written about him or whatever she has heard. She draws from them the sap of life and passes it on to all her members.

7. The 'fruit of this belly', therefore, is this life-giving food of the heart, and the result of this food is spiritual well-being.* Yes, the fruit of the belly is the healing of all disease, the strengthening of health, spiritual support and long continuance of life. In a word, its fruit is the fruit of the blessed contemplation of Jesus, namely, of 'the child'.* Every 'woman, when she is in labor, has sorrow,'* since she yearns to see the child whom she loves from her very depths, yet she is not able to bring forth what she desires. Her energy is not enough to bring the child to birth, and she falls back on herself defeated. But when finally the long labor is over, and the birthday of the promised child has dawned at last, then the woman will sing in celebration: 'A child is born to us and a son is given to us.'* Yet it is very rarely that women are able to bring forth this blessed fruit of a holy belly. It is only those to whom this grace is given, so that they can say with the apostle: 'We see in a mirror and in shadows.'* And also: 'But we all, with unveiled face, beholding the glory of the Lord, are being changed into his likeness, from one degree of glory to another.'*

That fruit, then, is the Lord's enjoyment of divine love, a kind of happy tasting in advance of eternal glory, a glorious transformation, as the apostle says, into the likeness of God.* Splendid indeed is this bud, and glorious is the fruit of this land,* but we have been told (not having been given the grace of experiencing it to the same degree),

Cf. Richard of St. Victor, Benjamin Minor I.3; PL 196:66D.

Cf. Jn 16:21

Ibid.

Is 9:6

1 Co 13:12

2 Co 3:18

Cf. 2 Co 3:18

Cf. Is 4:2

that there is great difficulty in bringing it forth, and very great and toilsome care is needed to foster it. It is a most delicate plant, and it refuses to dwell except for the spouse alone, among the lilies. It considers there is no holiness or happiness except in seeking, tasting and breathing in only those things that are found with the spouse. So, unless 'encompassed with lilies',* it cannot endure the things of this earth at all. They seem to be 'dung',* for it is living only in the things of heaven.*

Sg 7:2

Cf. Ph 3:8
Cf. Ph 3:20

But he who has blessed his bride's belly so that it may bring forth such a Son, must give her too the breasts she needs to feed him with her milk. Having filled her womb, it is only right he should at once fill her breasts so that the baby may sit on her lap and know at once the sweetness of her milk.

8. It follows logically that this praise of the belly should be followed by that of the breasts,* 'Your two breasts', says the spouse, 'are like two fawns, twins of a gazelle.'† But to discuss this more fully needs more weighty treatment so as to build you up in charity, and even more so as to praise the church', but most of all so as to glorify the spouse,

**Cf. Gregory the Great, Moralia 24.8.17; PL 76:295CD.*
†Sg 7:3

only Son of the Father, who reigns
with the Father and
the Holy Spirit,
God, for ever
and ever.
Amen.

The beginning of the seventy-second sermon.
Of the two breasts of the church, which take the shape of mercy and truth, after the pattern of the spouse's breasts. Of the many sets of gazelle twins, that is, of twin virtues, with which the soul loves Jesus with tender affection, is accustomed to feed fruit of its contemplation, having conceived it by his spouse.

'YOUR TWO BREASTS are like two fawns, twins of a gazelle.'*

Sg 7:3

Cf. 1 K 1:3

If you want to apply these words of the spouse to the Shulamite,* that is, to the church that will be united to Christ at the end of time, the meaning of 'breasts' can be clearly seen in what the apostle says. For on that day, mercy and truth will meet in the Shulamite's breasts, like the twin fawns of a gazelle.* Obviously, it is these two qualities, by the grace of the Holy Spirit, that were found in the bosom of the primitive church. They were like two breasts, giving suck to the whole church in its infancy, and that church came both from the circumcised and the uncircumcised. 'I tell you', says the apostle, 'that Christ became a servant to the circumcised, to show God's truthfulness, in order to confirm the promises given to the patriarchs; moreover, in order that the gentiles might

Sg 7:3

glorify God for his mercy.'* To establish this,   *Rm 15: 8,9*
he makes use of the testimony he finds in the
law and the prophets, laying bare breasts that
have been unapproachable for so long, and
offering milk from them to his little ones. For
Paul claimed that he was indebted to both,
that is, 'from those who were under the law,
and from those who were without the law.'*   *1 Co 9:21*
Like a loving nurse, he strove to adapt himself, in every way, to the small size of both,
so as to have both [for Christ].

2. By the special choice of the Holy Spirit,
Paul was set apart to be sent as apostle to the
gentiles.* Then, immediately afterwards,† he   **Cf. 1 Co 9:22*
was brought by the spouse into the wine   *†Cf. Ac 9:18*
cellar,* where charity was set in order in   *Cf. Sg 2:4*
him* and he became 'all things to all   *Cf. Sg 2:4*
men.'* This meant that he was richly en-   *Cf. 1 Co 9:22*
dowed with both breasts of charity for Jew as
well as gentile. You will say, perhaps, that
according to the interpretation Paul gave
these breasts in his preaching, they ought
rather to be described as 'the breasts of the
spouse.' Indeed, as far as I am concerned, I
do not deny it, but from the spouse's 'full-
ness',* Paul received these breasts also. For   *Cf. Jn 1:16*
where could he have found this mother's
heart, this mother's breasts, except as a gift
from the Father of mercies* and the God   *Cf. 2 Co 1:3*
of truth?

O good Jesus, what an abundance of the
sweetest, whitest milk there is in these breasts
of yours, which breathe forth the scent of
choicest balm! How richly, from this abundance, you have filled the breasts of our
mothers! At one time, Paul gently attracts the

Jews, speaking of God's mercy, and at another he tenderly draws the gentiles, speaking of God's truth. Hence both may enter simultaneously through the one door of faith, and 'altogether, with one voice' they may give honor to 'the God and Father of our Lord Jesus Christ.'* How does he do it? Not even Paul himself could give full expression to the greatness of this motherly love of his, but equally, he had not the least wish to present it as other than it was. 'God is my witness', he says, 'how I yearn for you all in the inmost heart of Christ Jesus.'*

3. O invaluable tenderness, which he surrendered to God alone to be valued! What but an excessive tenderness could have caused in Paul's heart that great grief and continual sorrow, which he calls upon the Spirit to witness is present?* So great was this tender love that it wounded Paul's heart and blazed within his inmost depth, so that he could much more truly be considered as mad from too much love than from too much learning!* Surely we can only think of it as some kind of madness or insanity when he desired, for the sake of his brothers' salvation, 'to be anathema to Christ'?* Just a short while before, he had declared nothing could separate him from that love, 'neither death nor life nor things present nor things to come, nor any created thing',* either in heaven or beneath the heavens. So then, is not Paul himself allowing love for his children or his brothers to do, or to try to do, what is not possible for any creature? On this occasion, completely carried away into ecstatic self-forgetfulness,

our Benjamin* was too immoderate for our   *Cf. Rm 11:1*
capacity. Of course, he was speaking here to
himself and to God. To us, who are indisputably babes and sucklings, this cry is the
cry of a man who is intoxicated or of a soul
taken up into ecstasy, not to say that of a
madman.

4. But what of it? Surely that tenderness
came down to him from that vein of tenderness which 'made him, who knew no sin, into
sin for our sake, so that we might be made the
justice of God in him'?* Surely to be made   *2 Co 5:21*
sin, to be made accursed, is to be 'anathema'?*   *Rm 9:3*
Yes, the dew of Hermon, which is what 'ana-
thema' means, came down on the mountain
of Zion,* and by it the church is cleansed   *Cf. Ps 133:3*
from sin, and the stream of cursing became
for her the dew of blessing. That is why,
Lord Jesus, as often as 'my soul is disturbed
within me'* because of the evils I have done   *Ps 42:6*
and the anathema I have deserved, I shall
remember your anathema, which, with such
indescribable love, you underwent for my
sake. I repeat, I shall remember you 'from the
land of Hermon, the lowly mountain',* in   *Ibid.*
other words, from your most humble state of
being 'lifted up'.* I remember how often you   *Cf. Jn 12:32*
recalled that it was on the cross that you had
to be 'lifted up', describing your self-empty-
ing, your 'kenosis', as your 'being lifted up'.

So, if I am not mistaken, you yourself,
Lord Jesus, are that gazelle (if I may venture
so to speak), to whose twin fawns you chose
to compare your bride's breasts. Yet, why
should I hesitate to say it, when I am sup-
ported by the authority of the bride herself?

The Holy Spirit, speaking through her mouth, not only calls you by this name, but even uses it as a term of tenderness, gently coaxing you and drawing you with love. 'My beloved is like a gazelle, the fawn of the deer.'* And again: 'Return, my beloved,' she says, 'Be like a gazelle, the fawn of the deer.'* At the very end of the song, too: 'Make haste, my beloved, and be like a gazelle, like a young stag on the mountains of spice.'* So, Lord God of power and might, although your majesty far exceeds a name of such lowliness, your dignity does not reject it, all the same.*

The gazelle is distinguished among all animals for its speed and its sight, one of which qualities can be interpreted as meaning mercy, and the other as truth. Indeed, 'your Word runs swiftly',* when you run in advance, to anticipate with the speed of unexpected grace, the sinner, whom you justify, or the just man, whom you sanctify. Yet you have a wonderful and terrible power of sharp sightedness, for you can gaze into the depths of the conscience; not only do you expose what is hidden, but you can even foresee what is still to be hidden. But, when you look upon the just, your eyes are all serene. By the light of your truth, you delicately make your way into the souls of those who love you, and your entry fills them with light.*

And indeed, in the former sense, your beloved demands that you make yourself like a gazelle, in as much as it may return to her with its usual gladness. It is as if she were to say: 'Return, my beloved',* but I beg you, do not be slow in returning, do not stand still, do not seize eagerly at digressions whenever possible. In a word, use the same speed of movement with which, to my grief, you have sometimes turned and run away from me, and now, return, my beloved, and run back to me. So we have a witness in the bride, and a still greater witness in the Holy Spirit, that the spouse is a gazelle.

5. When the spouse compares the twin fawns of this gazelle to the breasts of his bride, I think there is something he wants to make clear to us. It is this: her breasts are like his own breasts, and the bride has modeled her mercy and truth on the pattern of her spouse. Clearly, mercy and truth, which we said above were symbolized by speed of movement and keenness of sight, find no difficulty in expressing the same symbol in the gazelle's twin fawns. The one difference is that by the tenderness of their infant years, the tenderness of mercy is given fuller expression, and there is a gentle emphasis on the lovableness of truth. So it is beautiful and fitting that the bride's disposition should be likened to these dispositions of the spouse, since it is from them that she derives her attitude of mercy and the spirit of truth.

From the Spirit of mercy she receives the power to hasten to those who are still begrimed with worldly habits, so as to snatch them 'out of the pit of misery and out of the miry bog'.* By her compassion for them, by her entreaties, by imploring God for them in prayer, she mercifully forestalls those who do not ask for mercy, in fact, who even reject it.

Ps 40:2

 John of Ford

Cf. Ps 119:30

Cf. Sir 1:16,
Ps 111:10

Cf. Lk 23:34

Then, in the Spirit of truth, she shows them the way of truth,* humbly recommending the fear of the Lord, which is the beginning of wisdom,* in other words, is the milk of little children. Yes, because mercy is in the merciful God who pities those who 'do not know',* it is typical of it to seize on the ungrateful, to draw the unwilling, and, uncovering the bosom of its tenderness, to lay bare to them the nipple of its tender and motherly compassion. Moreover, it is typical of truth, since it proclaims God's justice and foretells his judgement, to admit them to the taste of the fear of God, as if from the breast of truth.

Consequently, if anyone prefers to think, as some of the fathers of the church did, that the 'two breasts of the bride' should be taken as the two testaments, here too there is an easy meaning as to why they are compared to the twin fawns of a gazelle. It is from the same breast of wisdom that both covenants flow, and it is the same bosom of truth that brings forth breasts to nourish the tender infancy of the suckling church. But, as we have just explained, the wisdom of God and the truth, which is Christ, are each called gazelle, which the bride says her beloved resembles and which she seeks to resemble herself.

6. Furthermore, it is obvious why these fawns are said to be twins, since they are always together, as if united by an equal relationship of blood, and in the mouth of these two witnesses, God has left an irrefutable testimony of the truth.* 'For in this

Cf. Mt 18:16

is the saying proved true,' says the Lord, that
'it is one who sows and another who
gathers,'* which means exactly the same as: *Jn 4:37*
'In the mouth of two witnesses, every word'
stands,* since those who speak are different   *Mt 18:16*
and what they speak is not different. So these
fawns, under the direction of our mother,
God's Wisdom, indulge themselves meanwhile,
and make their childhood delightful, through
the agency of the church and her bosom,
'until the day breathes and the shadows
flee,'* which means, until the veil of sym-   *Sg 2:17*
bols and sacraments is removed, and naked
truth reveals her face.

But then the heaven, which at present is
stretched out like a piece of parchment,*   *Cf. Ps 104:2*
will be rolled up like a scroll, as Isaiah puts
it,* which Paul interprets as meaning that,   *Cf. Is 34:4*
prophecies having passed away and tongues
being stilled, knowledge will come to an
end.* In fact, only the book of life will be   *1 Co 13:8*
unrolled before the eyes of all, in other words,
the blissful contemplation of Jesus' face. For
then 'they will all be taught by God,'* and   *Jn 6:45*
'the Only Son, who is in the bosom of the
Father,' he will make him known,* and   *Jn 1:18*
speak to us plainly of the Father.*   *Jn 16:25*

This interpretation of the bride's breasts,
therefore, holds good if we take the bride as
the church, either the church that was wedded
to Christ in the early days of the faith, or the
church which is wedded to him today, or the
church which will wed him at the end of
time, formed from the remnant of Israel.

7. But, on the other hand, this description
may be addressed to some soul, to whom

<table>
<tr><td>Ph 1:21</td><td>'to live is Christ,'* who finds it easy to say, in the Holy Spirit: 'My beloved is mine and</td></tr>
<tr><td>Sg 2:16</td><td>I am his.'* But in that case it remains true</td></tr>
</table>

'to live is Christ,'* who finds it easy to say, in the Holy Spirit: 'My beloved is mine and I am his.'* But in that case it remains true that anybody of this nature, since she is a bride, is a mother and has breasts. Obviously, if any soul at all, who does the will of the Father, is Jesus' mother,* as he himself says, then this is much more so here. This soul has full access to her heavenly spouse, she has become fruitful from his holy embraces, and without any doubt at all, she has conceived and given birth in the Holy Spirit. Moreover, to pursue what was said in the previous sermon, the son who is born to her,* is the fruit of divine contemplation. In the appearance of this child, the mother who labored to give him birth, rejoices in proportion to her previous suffering, over the coming into the world of a new man,* and the springing up of truth from the earth.* God, who gave her the child, must of necessity grant her breasts; he made her womb fruitful, he will also make her breasts full. He says, therefore: 'Your two breasts are like two fawns, twins of a gazelle.'*

We would not be on safe ground if we tried to explain this gazelle by wandering away from the bride's understanding of it, which we spoke of above, or if we looked for a meaning, other than the beloved. But when it comes to the two identical fawns, it is possible to be uncertain as to which meaning the spouse wanted to be understood. In fact, this gazelle has innumerable fawns, as well as having many pairs of twins. The spirit of wisdom and understanding is one pair of twins, the spirit of counsel and fortitude is yet another, and the spirit of knowledge and piety is still a third.* It is only the spirit of fear that has no twin companions with it, because its beginnings come short of perfection. But maybe reverential fear, which is set on the topmost peak of wisdom, ought to correspond with its direct opposite, beginners' fear, which is placed at virtues' foot. What one kind of fear begins, the other brings to completion.*

Likewise, when Wisdom opened his mouth in the hearing of his disciples, and enumerated the beatitudes in successive stages, like a gazelle, he brought forth his offspring in twins, pairing off the merits of different virtues and their rewards. In plain words, he gave the kingdom of heaven to the poor in spirit,* he promised the earth to the meek† and comfort to the mourners,* and he vowed that those who hungered and thirsted for justice would have their fill.* He said that the merciful would obtain mercy,* he pledged the vision of God to the pure of heart,* he honored peacemakers with the title of divine sonship,* and established as kings of heaven those who suffer persecution for justice' sake.*

8. And there are very many other similar pairs of 'twins', as anyone who seeks, may easily discover, either in the shade of the wood,* that is, in the mysterious darkness of holy scripture, or even in the open stretches of the plains. Clearly, wisdom and prudence are born twins, the first of which is active in the practice of virtue, while Job defines prudence as 'to depart from evil'.* Understanding

Cf. Is 11:2

Cf. Sir 1:14

**Mt 5:3*
†Mt 5:5
**Mt 5:4*

Mt 5:6

Mt 5:7

Mt 5:8

Mt 5:9

Mt 5:10

Cf. Ezk 31:8

Jb 28:18

Pr 4:25
Cf. Ps 119:128

Ps 85:10
Jn 1:17

and performance are also a pair of twins, since, as Solomon says, we should look before we leap,* and the understanding is sharpened, in its turn, by having obeyed.* Again, the heart is purified by faith and grows in insight, while, on the other hand, understanding illuminates faith; equally, too, understanding and feeling affect and enlighten each other. Then, an outstanding set of twins is love of God and love of our neighbor, and each is bound closely to the other in achieving their design. 'Mercy and truth', the psalmist tells us, 'will meet each other' in the business of saving men, and 'justice and peace will embrace,'* while John bears witness that 'grace and truth came through Jesus Christ.'* But who could possibly count out all the different kinds of virtue, or rather, who could possibly explain, among so many different pairs of twins, which of them the spouse chose as a comparison for the breasts of his bride? To go into all this would be a lengthy and difficult matter, unless perhaps it was his intention to compare her breasts to every single one of them!

9. So it seems to me that here the bride is being praised for her prudence, she yearns to contemplate her beloved and has deserved to perceive the fruit of this contemplation, however tiny, because of her prudence. She nurses it in her bosom, and has made a practice of giving it milk, first from her tendency to some virtues, and then from her tendency to others. Taught by her beloved, she sees in her meditations, that meritorious actions and their rewards go in pairs. The more she is

stirred to any virtues, the more she ponders the rewards of these virtues. The more quickly she grasps their blessedness, the more unceasingly does she direct her mind to the purity of these virtues.

In short, if you think carefully over all we have said above, these pairs of twins are divided into two kinds: that is, virtue is repaid by being simply its own reward, or it is crowned with the prize of glory. You have one pair of twins when grace is given because grace is there, and the saints, as the psalmist sings, go from virtue to virtue.* The other kind is when the Lord gives grace and glory, and repays every virtue individually with the same recompense of blessedness. In both kinds, then, the bride is tirelessly engaged, pondering with eager attention the stages of virtue, the chain of grace, and the eternal recompense, until he who was born of her is weaned from her breasts, there breathes the day* that knows no setting,† and she is taken into the region of eternal light, the country of the Father of lights, to the glory and honor

Ps 84:7

**Cf. Sg 2:17*
†Cf. Easter vigil hymn, Exullet

of her spouse, the Father's only Son,
who with the Father and
the Holy Spirit, lives
and reigns, God,
for ever and
ever.
Amen.

The beginning of the seventy-third sermon.
How 'ivory tower' is a commendation of the
outstanding humility of the Lord's mother, as
well as of the glory of her virginity. Next, how
the same phrase is in praise of the church's
humility, and the threefold praise of the neck
is a commendation of three forms of humility.

Sg 7:4

'YOUR NECK IS LIKE an ivory tower.'*
This terse phrase has a very special
relevance to the Lord's mother. There
may indeed be queens in their thousands, all
of whom have been privileged to enjoy, here
on earth, the embraces of Jesus, our Solomon,* but 'there is one who is the chosen
of her mother, of the woman who bore her.'*
She stands at the right hand of the King of
glory,* and sits down beside him too, cleaving
to him without intermediary. She is the
holiest of virgins, the most fruitful of mothers,
the happiest of women. And throughout this
whole song, all the praise has her in view,
first and foremost, because of the unique
privilege which she has from the Holy Spirit,
and this is specially so when it is the bride
who is being addressed or referred to. But in
this particular verse, it is extremely clear that
praise of the Lord's mother has, if I may so
put it, been thrust unavoidably into our

Cf. Sir 47:12-17
Sg 6:8

Cf. 1 K 22:19

hands, so that it would be both imprudent and unpermissible for us to be secretly anxious to turn aside from it.

2. For what could be more obvious than that the outstanding humility of the Lord's glorious mother is being praised,* when the bride's 'neck' is compared to an ivory tower? Then, the fact of the tower's being called 'ivory' means that admiration of her most noble virginity is added to wonder at her exceptional humility. Who could not immediately see the reference to the glory of this most radiantly white of virtues? Ivory is the most precious of all bones, which the Lord fashioned for her in secret.* He hid it away carefully from the prince of this world,* who was to be deceived by it and brought to destruction.*

In a previous verse of the song, this modesty was praised by the spouse by a reference to the bride's 'navel', which he compared to a rounded bowl.* Equally, 'belly' was a symbol for the fruitfulness by which, while nature stood in awe, this virgin mother brought forth God and man, and 'breasts' for the devotion and tenderness of this submissive mother.* It seems to me that a woman's two breasts indicate here two kinds of tenderness, so that she ministered to the Lord Jesus as to her own child, the virgin's son, the fruit of her womb, and also provided for the same Jesus as for the Lord of the angels, the Son of the most High, acting now as the Lord's handmaid.* So, if the tenderness of the virgin mother was twofold in this way, there were also two ways in which she regarded the twofold nature of

Cf. Bernard, Miss. 1,5; SBOp 4:17; CF 18:9f.

Cf. Ps 139:15

Jn 12:31

Cf. Lk 10:18

Cf. Sg 7:2

Cf. Sg 7:3

Cf. Lk 2:38

Cf. Sg 7:3

the Word made flesh from her: in that personal or hypostatic union, she both lovingly adored and reverently embraced him. This is why this wisest of virgins was given by the spouse the appropriate name of 'gazelle'.* Above all other saints, she had the privilege of contemplating most keenly the glory of the only Son of the Father, and she outran them all in the incomparable earnestness of her charity. So she is a symbol of serenity because of the deep gaze of her contemplation, yet a symbol of allegiance because of her swiftly moving charity.

But, after these virtues have been commended, it is only right that 'tower of ivory' should be added, in praise of her humility. Surely it is a wonderful thing that, with God, a soul enriched with so many great virtues as to surpass all the saints, should in the end transcend her own self by her over-surpassing humility. So, as we have said, before all else, this beautiful description refers to the blessed Mother of the Lord, but, with all respect for her special dignity, it will also be in order to extend this praise to the Lord's bride, that is, the church, under the same heading.

3. First of all, we must say why we have called 'neck' or 'tower' a symbol of humility. 'Neck' is an obvious enough symbol of the humble soul, since we are accustomed to bow it when we are coming forward submissively, when we are bending in devout adoration, or when we are humbly obeying.* On the contrary, a stiff neck, a rigid and unyielding position of the head, usually denotes the hard, unbending pride of the wicked. In

Cf. RB 7.63

short, scripture says of Leviathan: 'His
strength will abide in his neck.'* Yes, indeed,   *Jb 41:13*
as it says in another place, he is very proud,
and his pride is continually ascending,* and   *Cf. Ps 74:23*
not even the terrible and eternal heat of hell
fire can make it bend. And again, Isaiah has
this to say of the daughters of Zion; 'Because
the daughters of Zion are haughty, and walk
with outstretched neck, . . . the Lord will
shave the heads of Zion's daughters and strip
away their hair.'* In this verse, a terrible   *Is 3:26*
rebuke is issued against certain nominal
daughters of the church, because of their
pride. Since they do not know how to bend
the neck, either in prayer to God or in obedience, they are to be shamed with baldness
as if they were lepers and they are to be
denuded, by God's decree, of the false
appearance of the virtues that adorn them
like locks of hair, and at the end, all men will
see it.

Again, it is for this reason that scripture
says of wisdom that it has trampled with its
own power on the necks of the proud and
lofty.* This is unmistakably seen to have   *Cf. Magnificat*
been fulfilled when the very Wisdom of God   *antiphon for Satur-*
'reached from end to end',† from the 'end'   *day Vespers before*
of the heights of majesty to the 'end' of the   *the first Sunday of*
                                                August in the Cister-
depths of humility, and with the foot of his   *cian liturgy.*
own power, which is humility, he overthrew,   *†Cf. Wis 8:1*
cast down and put to shame all the stiff rigor
of inflated pride. It is called his own special
power, but Wisdom, in his charity, handed on
to his disciples, by word and deed, the
discipline of this power. 'Learn of me,' he
said, 'because I am meek and humble of

Mt 11:29

heart.'* He did not say: Learn of me, so that you may be meek and humble of heart. That is what some teachers must be thought of as saying, when they give a magnificent discourse on humility, teachers who speak and do not act. But Jesus says: 'Learn by me that I am meek and humble of heart',* so that what you cannot grasp just in my bare words, you may fully grasp by the example of my greatness having bowed itself low.

4. Very appropriately, before these words he has said: 'Take my yoke upon you',* for the neck that is bent with the willing humility of Christ, finds that the yoke is not heavy now, but light.* Why do you think this yoke lies so 'heavily on all the sons of Adam, from the day when they leave their mother's womb until the day' of their death,* if not because of pride? From the very breast their necks have started to swell up with the thick fat of arrogance. Immediately, then, they come under the yoke, which cannot at all be thrown off or broken, and perhaps in this way, so heavily weighed down by the yoke of servitude, the race of Adam may learn not to stiffen their necks and bear their heads on high.

But this way of teaching or learning is extraordinarily severe, because it can wear the neck away and actually rot it, but only in the slightest degree, if that, make it bend. So the Son of God came to bear and pull our yoke along with us, and the result was that it was the yoke that rotted away, in the presence of the holy oil.* He endowed us with the Holy Spirit as well as drawing us by his example, so that we might pull this yoke in humble fellowship. His fellowship, his holy oil anointing us, make the yoke light.* Through Christ's grace, the punishment of pride now becomes the mark of humility, and the forced imposition of humiliation has become a freely chosen humility. In other words, the yoke of Adam has been changed into the yoke of Christ, and so it is now an honor, not a burden; it raises us up instead of casting us down, it builds us up instead of undermining us.

5. Yes, the spouse is indeed speaking to a woman whose 'nard gives forth its fragrance',* when he says: 'Your neck is like a string of beads.'* And again, after signaling out her adornments, he brings in an oblique reference to the strength and excellence of her humility, also, by saying: 'Your neck is like David's tower, built with ramparts.'* And then he goes on to remark on her beauty and dignity, as well as her intrepidity: 'Your neck is like an ivory tower.'* So first of all, humility, the mother of all virtues, adorns the soul with meekness and modesty.* Secondly, it strengthens it by patience and lifts it up, through contempt for things of earth and hope for things of heaven. And lastly, through a very pure contemplation of its spouse, humility makes it the bride of the Word of God.

But listen while I put this more plainly. By praising the bride's neck three separate times, the spouse seems to me to be pointing out to us three different kinds of humility. There is, in fact, humility in her own regard, humility

*Cf. Mt 11:29.
Cf. Bernard SC 42.7;
SBOp 2:37;
CF 7:215.*

Sg 1:11

Sg 1:9

Sg 4:4

Sg 7:4

**Cf. Gregory,
Moralia 23.13.24
& 34.23.51,
PL 76:265B;
747A.*

Bernard, Gra 3.6;
SBOp 3:20;
CF 13:34.

with regard to her neighbor, and humility with regard to God.* The first is in truly recognizing what she is, the second in compassionating and giving due respect to her neighbor, and the third is in very humbly contemplating God.

The first is found when everyone individually thinks humbly of himself, whether in his good deeds or his bad. Like holy Job, he feels afraid of all he has done,* repenting of his evil deeds, but making little of his good. I think it is of this kind of humility that it is said: 'Your neck is like a string of beads.'* It seems to me that there is deliberate use made of a plural word: 'string of beads', because she is lovingly pondering both good and bad, and from this she becomes adorned with an understanding of humility. From this she barricades the breast of her soul, as if with beads of gold, safeguarding her purity as well as defending her self-restraint. This is why, because there are these two kinds of beads, the bride immediately after receives from her spouse a twofold acclamation of her title to beauty. 'Behold, you are beautiful, my love,' he says, 'behold you are beautiful.'*

In the gospel, the most merciful of all fathers runs tenderly to meet his son, coming from a faroff country, and we are told that he 'fell upon his neck'.* What he was embracing so thankfully was undoubtedly his son's humility, which had at long last brought him back to himself, after having devoured his substance with harlots.* If this is how God accepts the humility of a soul who repents of his shameful sins, think how he must

Cf. Jb 9:28

Sg 1:9

Sg 1:14

Cf. Lk 15:20

Cf. Lk 15:13

delight in one whose heart, aware of nothing
with which to reproach itself,* feels anxious
even about its good deeds! 'Even though I am
innocent,' says the innocent man, 'my soul
takes no account of that, and I feel weary of
my life.'* And 'I am not aware of anything
with which to reproach myself',* that great
friend of God, Paul, was not afraid to say, and
yet he did not dare to glory in the testimony
of his conscience without a tremor of anxiety.*

So the bride's neck is rightly said to be like
a string of beads,* since she has gained the
favor of her most humble spouse by adorning
herself, as described above, with two kinds
of humility. It is to this that scripture is
referring when it says: 'He resists the proud
but gives grace to the humble.'*

6. Next, there is humility in relation to
Christ, there is no virtue or excellence that
it does not contain.* Scripture describes it at
the time when Jesus humbled himself before
John, and that humble servant trembled at
the abasement of such greatness and majesty.*
Jesus' answer was: 'Leave it like this for the
time being, for it is fitting that we should, in
this way, do all that righteousness demands.'*
He called this humility 'all righteousness' in
two senses. Through it, the spotless Lamb of
God,* as if he was in need of sanctification,
sought baptism from a servant, and the
servant, too, acknowledging the Lord of
majesty, did not let this overwhelming honor
make him refuse the service of his loyal
obedience. Indeed, it is with this humility
that all kingdoms are ruled, all kingship
exercised, all teaching imparted, all

Cf. 1 Co 4:4

Jb 9:21

1 Co 4:4

Cf. 1 Co 4:4

Cf. Sg 1:10

Jm 4:6

Cf. Bernard, O Epi 4; SBOp 4:311.

Cf. Mt 3:13

Mt 3:15

Cf. Jn 1:36

religion made holy.

Humility like this, then is well compared to David's tower,* 'on which hang a thousand shields'* and the armor of the warriors, because the armor of obedience, as saint Benedict, teacher of the obedient tells us, is very beautiful and very strong.* We have the incontrovertible witness of the most perfect of the Fathers, that obedience is the quickest way to reach the heights of perfection and to win a complete victory over spiritual and bodily passions. It seems to me this is symbolized by there being a thousand shields, since this is a perfect number and it indicates the progress of hearts made perfect.

7. But the tower is called 'David's', whether David son of Jesse or David Son of God. In fact, this was, or rather is, the tower of them both, for it is founded upon solid rock,* and stands immovable and impregnable. I call it the tower of both Davids, but there is a difference.

Certainly, David, son of Jesse, built for himself a tower of invincible humility, so that he would never be calumniated by the proud* and never surrender to the lies of the arrogant.* This is why, since he feared the calumnies of the proud, he begged God: 'Keep me as the apple of your eye from those who fight against your right hand.'* Those who 'fight against your right hand' is his name for the spirit of pride or proud men, for scripture is referring to them when it says: 'God fights against the proud',* and he seeks, in every way possible, to keep himself clean from their unclean touch. Moreover, David began to

Cf. Sg 4:4

Sg 4:4

RB Prol. 3

Cf. Mt 7:25

Cf. Ps 119:122

Cf. Ps 119:121

Ps 17:8-9

Jm 4:6

build this tower for himself even from his
boyhood years, when he was chosen out
of his brothers, by reason of his humility,
and a proud reigning monarch had been
rejected.* Then, after his kingly consecra- *Cf. 1 S 15:26*
tion, he served his father as usual and went
off to pasture the sheep, patiently enduring
the jeers of his brothers and disarming their
jealousy. Consequently, he breathed forth,
not the unction of kingly consecration, but
only the scent of gentleness and humility.
Later, too, despite his glorious triumph over
Goliath, and despite his having repeatedly
conquered and routed the foe, his construction of this great building never ceased. On
the contrary (and this was the most glorious
victory of them all), amid these deeds of
valor, he triumphed over the spirit of self-
conceit, so that from a pure conscience, he
could confidently sing to God: 'Lord, my
heart is not proud, nor exalted my eyes.'* *Ps 131:1*
And again: 'O Lord, remember David and all
his meekness.'* *Ps 132:1*

Is there any reason why we, and anyone
who has come to admire and imitate David's
humility, should not grasp with outstretched
hand the shields hanging from this tower,* *Cf. Sg 4:4*
whenever the spirit of vainglory attacks us?
Why should we not arm ourselves by the
example of this great hero, and borrow from
him a meek heart and a humble way of
speech? Yet, all the same, it is from the tower
of the other David, whose heart was in
accord with the heart of God,* that the hands *Cf. 1 S 13:14*
of the strong can more easily reach this armor.
The humility of the Lord of glory is, in

proportion, far more wonderful than the earlier David, who, if considered objectively, was very sinful and 'doomed to death'.* In fact, David was fully subject to corruption and worms.*

8. But when we come to the Lord of power and might, the King of glory, we find that his humility surpasses all our capacity for admiration. Although 'he was in the form of God,'* he went through all the conditions of human wretchedness, even to paying the forfeit of death. Then, just like David, he submitted himself most obediently to his parents,* indeed, far more than David ever did, and it was his preference to be the servant of his disciples rather than receive from them the service of servants.* Finally, how very humbly he called sinners to repentance, promising not only that they would be forgiven, but that they could enter the kingdom of heaven.* He revealed himself to them as wholly meek and humble,* offering to heal their wounds with oil. He proclaimed that even though they were still far off, among the heathen, the Father of mercy would come running to meet them,* and at the very first moment of their coming, what we could call a feast in honor of their new life from the dead* would be in readiness for them.* Then there is the fact that, at the end of his life, He himself adopted the cause of sinners by sacrificing his most holy body, and offered a stainless Lamb to God his Father on behalf of their stains.*

Therefore, as we said before, humility is the special virtue of true Wisdom, made man for us, and through this power, he has trampled on the neck of the proud and arrogant, whether they are demons or men. This is what the Song is saying, though in other words, when this same virtue is called: 'tower of David.'*

Cf. Sg 7:4

9. The humility of the bride, meaning here the church or any soul that loves God, could receive no higher commendation than to be compared to the humility of Christ, that incomparable humility. Yet, when I say 'compared', I mean only that there is a certain likeness, not an equality. For who could find the words to describe its pre-eminence? Christ sits now at the right hand of the majesty of God,* and yet, just as if he were really David's son, raised on high and consecrated king, he devotes himself to his former task of tending sheep in his Father's land.* When he ascended to his Father, he did not 'leave us orphans',* but proclaimed that his dearest delight was to be with the children of men.* Moreover, he accepts gifts from men,* and anyone who receives one of his little ones in his name, he thinks of as having received him.*

Cf. Heb 1:3

Cf. 2 S 7:8
Cf. Jn 14:18

Cf. Pr 8:31
Cf. Ps 68:18

Cf. Mt 18:5

All this refers to the bride's humility, in regard to men.

10. But as for the humility which related to her spouse, we remember having compared it to an 'ivory tower', or rather, that this was the comparison the spouse made himself, by saying: 'Your neck is like an ivory tower.'* This tower has this very precious kind of material in its construction, and no soul, poor as it is, can possibly provide it. For, as the gospel says, anyone that wants to build a tower like this, first sits down to

Sg 7:4

Cf. Lk 14:28

work out if he has enough material to finish it.* It is tragic to think how many have begun, and then run short of material, a laughing stock to those who say: 'This man began to build and could not finish.'* How many we have often seen who, at the beginning of their conversion, dedicate themselves to holy meditation, batter heaven with their prayers, and, like the young Benjamin,* linger all day long in the bridal chamber with the bride. And yet, though I can hardly bear to say it, what they began in the Spirit, they finish in the flesh.* If they lack materials, as their poverty proves, why do they not run to the Father of all spirits,* why do they not beg him, in whose name they laid their foundations, to complete their work?

Lk 14:30

Cf. Ps 68:27

Cf. Gal 3:3

Cf. Heb 12:9

This ivory tower, then, in all its purity, is the contemplation of the greatness, wisdom and goodness of God. The spouse says 'ivory', and I have deliberately spoken of 'all its purity', since it is, of course, true that there are some, as the apostle says, who 'become futile in their thinking'* when they contemplate what is sublime. By claiming that they are wise, and that from their own stock they have plenty of material with which to build a tower of ivory, they reveal themselves as building more the tower of Babel.* They are raising a tower of brick, rather than ivory, a tower of pride and shame and not one of defense.

Rm 1:21

Cf. Gn 11:9

But the pure bride of Christ, lost in the contemplation of her spouse, gazes long at his majesty and prostrates herself completely before him, in humility of heart. She looks

wonderingly at Wisdom, and like the psalmist, she too suffers a certain ecstasy of mind, crying out: 'Your knowledge is too wonderful for me, it is too strong, I cannot reach it.'*   *Ps 139:6* When she gazes on the riches of his goodness and love, her heart cannot contain its wonder at them and she grows faint, realizing more and more her own nothingness. Look where she will into that inaccessible Light, she comes back to herself more humble, so that it is easy to understand that the bride of Christ is truly very rich. She can build a tower so precious, one that all the wise men of this present world, and all those, right up to modern times, who were sages in their own eyes, have started to build and at once come to grief. But they built with bricks, and, as scripture says, the bricks have fallen down.* And they   *Cf. Is 9:10* raised a tower to their own glory, but the bride to the glory of the Lord her God,
the only Son of the Father, who,
with the Father and the
Holy Spirit, lives and
reigns, God, for
ever and ever.
Amen.

SERMON SEVENTY-FOUR

The beginning of the seventy-fourth sermon. How 'heshbon' symbolizes a great throng of the repentant, especially those who are to be converted to the Lord at the end of time by the preaching of Israel. How 'the bride's eyes' describe the church's tender compassion and how she watches over our salvation, and they are compared to 'pools', because from their tenderness and their teaching, they offer a font for those who would be cleansed.

'YOUR EYES ARE LIKE pools in Heshbon, by the gate of the daughter of many.'*

Sg 7:4

First, we must look at Heshbon, to see what kind of city it was, and next, why the spouse chose to compare the bride's eyes to its pools. For it was a large city, well provided with gates, and from the very words used in this verse, it is clear that it is known as 'the daughter of many', meaning that it is rich in having many citizens. Moreover, the gates are not passed over in silence, since the pools are mentioned as having been 'at the gate'. In fact, there is a place in Isaiah, where a prophecy is woven against Moab, and there I read that the fall of this city will not take place without the prophet's repeated groans and tears. It speaks of the shouting and weeping

144

as if the city had already been destroyed: 'Heshbon and Elealeh have cried out, their voice is heard as far as Jahaz.'* And a little further on: 'Tell her wounds to those who laughed upon your walls of baked brick, for the meadows of Heshbon, the vineyards of Sabana, are desolate.'* And again: 'I will make you drunk with my tears, Heshbon and Elealeh.'*

Is 15:4

Is 16:7-8

Is 16:9

2. If you listen to these words very carefully, they contain a prophecy of the conversion and penitence of these same citizens, under the image of the city's destruction.* Once before, this kind of destruction was referred to: 'In forty days time, Nineveh will be destroyed!'* But the Lord changed his verdict, in his tenderness, and what happened was that, as scripture puts it, 'he made lightning bring forth the rain.'* He destroyed the city of the Ninevites—by converting it! Solomon sums it up: 'Convert the sinner, and he is no longer there.'* It was in this manner that the innocent man, taking upon himself the sorrow of a repentant soul, called down the destruction of his own day: 'May the day on which I was born, perish, and the night on which it was said: A man has been conceived.'* Then a little later, he says to himself, weeping, and re-emphasizing his prayer for his own destruction: Why did I not die in the womb, why did I not perish the minute I left it?'* Obviously, if these words are taken in their literal sense only, they sound like the complaints of a soul who will not suffer and who murmurs sinfully against God. But if we pierce through to the core of truth within

**Cf. Gregory, Hom. in Ezech. I.10.26; PL 76: 896D.*

Jon 3:4

Ps 134:7

Pr 12:9

Job 3:3

Job 3:11

them, they are the cries of the repentant, exclamations full of tenderness.

3. So, in that prophecy of Isaiah, which he calls 'the Burden of Moab' many things about this loving kind of destruction are very plainly and fully set out. He says they must be clothed in sackcloth,* that, 'on every head' there will be 'baldness', and 'every beard will be shorn,'* that 'all wailing will melt into tears,'* and that 'the soul of Moab will wail to itself.'* Then the prophet himself cannot conceal how much he is affected emotionally by compassion for such penitence, and exclaims: 'My heart cries out for Moab,'* and 'I will make you drunk with my tears, Heshbon and Elealeh,'* and 'My soul moans like a lyre for Moab.'* Finally, he shows the future effect of this repentance, and its greatness, when he says: 'Send forth the Lamb, O Lord, the ruler of the earth, from the rock of the desert to the mount of the daughter of Zion.'*

To explain all this in detail, at this point, would take a long time, but it may be enough to have mentioned briefly that these words of the prophet indicate the laborious work of repentance and show solicitude for the penitent; they make clear what great care must be used in hastening to those who repent, and what great tenderness must be used to help them. But, in the end, the humility of repentance gives rise to very great innocence or glory, as is prophesied by 'sending the Lamb from the rock of the desert to the mount of the daughter of Zion'.

In the first place, the 'baldness of the head'

and the 'shaving of the beard',* glorify the   *Cf. Is 15:2*
unfeigned zeal of confession. This strips the
head of its hair, that is, the heart of its evil
thoughts, as if a sharp razor had been laid to
it. The beard, too, that is, the presumptuous
strength of the will, is despoiled by the naked
disclosure of its wicked deeds. Clothing with
sackcloth follows,* that is, the harshness of a   *Cf. Is 15:2*
more austere life, to punish the previous
luxuriousness and subdue sexual desires. Yet,
'Moab cries for Moab, and the soul of Moab
wails for itself',* since waiting is the usual   *Cf. Is 16:7*
custom at a funeral or the burning of cities
or an enemies' devastation. Everyone urges
on their neighbor to lament, not only in word
and tongue, but by a tearful flood of sobbing.
So, in this kind of tenderness for the repentant, sinners have the gospel of repentance
preached to them by the penitent. Then
'anyone who hears, can say Come.'* It is   *Rv 22:17*
very much more effective to persuade people
to come by example, than to urge them on by
preaching.

4. Well, then, since Isaiah prophesied that
something like this was to happen in the city
of Heshbon, namely, the very last of Moab's
towns, it is this precise city that the spouse
now sets before us, by way of comparison, in
order to fashion from it a compliment for his
bride. Isaiah promised that he would make
this city drunk with his tears,* because to   *Cf. Is 16:9*
their tears of repentance, he would join his
own tears of compassion for them. He would
soothe the city's grief, as if with wine, by his
own pity. Consequently, 'Heshbon' means the
great throng of penitents who daily come

back to the Father of mercies through the ministry of the bride. Or else it means at least the throng which the bride of Christ, through the force of her preaching, will draw with her to the great marriage feast of joy, and this throng will be taken from Israel when time ends and she is finally reconciled. From this it easily follows that 'Heshbon' can be translated as 'meditation' or 'thoughts', but also as 'a girdle of grief'.*

As for this reflection or these thoughts, the second impression indicates their nature, showing that they arise from the sorrow which accompanies repentance, like the cry of that penitent soul who says, 'I will meditate on my sin, and my sin is always before me.'* And another contrite voice cries out: 'All my years I shall meditate on you in the bitterness of my soul.'* There is the same emotion behind this saying, too: 'The thoughts of men will confess to you, and the rest of their meditation will make a festival day for you.'* He says: 'they will make a festival day for you,' for the tears of the penitent make a celebration for the Lord, crowded with rejoicing citizens of heaven. The tenderest of all Fathers calls together his friends and neighbors from all sides,* so as to complete and heap high the happiness of this great feast of love.

5. On the other hand, to say that 'Heshbon' means 'a girdle of grief', is to take girdle of grief as the unchangeable intention of perseverance in contrition. It is in reference to this girdle that the repentant wear, that it is written in Isaiah, addressing the sinful soul:

**Jerome, Liber de nominibus hebraicus; PL 23:793; CC 76:81.*

Ps 38:18

Is 38:15

Ps 76:11

Cf. Lk 15:6

'You will have a rope for your girdle.'* And
there is much the same in Job: 'He loosens
the belts of kings, and binds their reins with a
cord.'* A rope or cord is substituted for a
girdle or belt, when the soul who takes a vain
delight in its virtue of chastity, has the source
of its pride snatched away from it and it is
supplied with matter for perpetual humility.
But it advances from this humble girdle of
grief to the girdle of strength, which the
strong woman uses to gird her loins* and keep
her chastity perpetually vigorous. If the spirit
of pride has brought her down to a humbler
state, equally, by God's mercy, will the spirit
of humility form her anew in the state from
which she fell.

So it is a true prophecy that the bride's
eyes will be like 'pools in Heshbon',* because
it means that the church, as we have said, feels
an eager, tender pity for the earnestness of
penitents, and like the inhabitants of heaven,
has a deep interior love for them. When Isaiah
says that Heshbon is to be made drunk with
his tears,* does it not seem to you that
those eyes were like 'pools of Heshbon'? It is
my belief that, even then, he beheld in a spirit
of prophecy, the throng of repentant sinners
who would come running from all sides. They
would run, clapping their hands and dancing,
as if to greet those hastening to a day of
solemn festival, now, at this very moment.
Surely he himself ran to greet them, since it
was he who in former times urged all and
sundry that they must greet them with bread
and water? His actual words were: 'All men
who live in the land of the south, go out

Is 21:14

to greet the fugitive with bread, run out to
bear water to the thirsty.'* Obviously, he
meant us to understand that 'the men who
live in the south' are those who accompany
the spouse or are companions of the bride, for
the Sun of divine love already shines warmly
upon them. For them, the north wind has already arisen and departed, and the gentler
south wind has already begun to blow. So
they are ordered to greet with bread and
water 'the fugitive', that is, the fearful and
trembling throng of penitent sinners. It is their
duty to serve them joyfully, from the great
store of their goods, namely, from the abundance of their hearts, whatever will build
them up and comfort them.

6. But a warning, or rather, instruction, is
also given, that Moab is to be a shelter for

Is 16:4

them from their destroyers,'* and the reason
must surely be, that those who have already
been privileged to experience in themselves
the merciful goodness of God, should be
found especially eager to have mercy on
others. As scripture says: 'Freely you have

Mt 10:8

received, freely give.'* Moreover, the bride has
rightly proclaimed that her spouse's name is

Cf. Sg 1:2

'oil poured out',* because pity, which comes
from heaven detests a selfish breast. It does
not know how to be closed up or restrained,
but like a spring of neverfailing oil, it exults to
break out and bubble forth. All it seeks is a
supply of great vessels so that it may flow
from one to the other.

Therefore, Moab, having found mercy and
now hiding from the face of wrath, is ordered
to be a refuge from the face of the destroyer

for the one who is in flight and for the one
seeking a hiding place, for, 'With you',
says the Lord, 'my fugitives will find a
home.'* It is as though he were telling
Moab: 'Ought not you to have compassion on your fellow servants, since I had
compassion on you?'* Therefore, open the
bosom of your tenderness to my fugitives,
fleeing from the sight of my wrath. Show
them the sanctuary of divine compassion,
where they may safely hide. So Moab
cries out for Moab, and Moab wails for
Moab, and Moab besieges and lays Moab
waste, joining with those who 'rejoice
upon walls of burnt brick', in other words,
who delight in the very worst circumstances. Heshbon, now destroyed, tells of
its wounds* (something we can see happening
every day in the church), because now that it
has been privileged to be drawn, it at once
begins to draw others. One who has recovered
from his own illness, has learned how to be
the servant, or even the doctor, to his sick
brother.

7. The bride's eyes, then, are like 'pools
in Heshbon';* in other words, they are tender
with pity and eager to provide help. But it is
by tears of sorrow that Heshbon arouses in
her a tenderness for her sins. It is only from
the spontaneous pity of the Lord's bride that
Heshbon learns the tenderness to pity herself.
Surely one who could beg the Lord: 'Who
will give water to my head and a fountain of
tears to my eyes, so that I may weep for the
dead of the daughter of my people?'*: surely
such a one had this kind of pool, or at least;

Is 16:4

Mt 18:33

Is 16:7

Sg 7:4

Jer 9:1

longed to have it? It is Jeremiah, a true priest of God, a true priest among priests, of whom scripture says: 'Here is one who prays much for the people and for the entire holy city of Jerusalem.'* And was not Isaiah very rich, a man who could give the cup of compassion to the city of Heshbon, a cup filled with his own tears, and make them drunk with it?*

It was Isaiah, too, who said: 'My soul moans for Moab like a lyre, and my heart for the wall of baked brick.'* 'By soul', he implied that his open and tender pity was breaking out, with unmistakable evidence, while 'heart' signifies the loving torments of hidden, interior grief. The soul, then, of any preacher who is full of tender love 'moans for Moab like a lyre,'* when he incites the the sinful soul to repentance and laments, with tears, our original fall and the ruin of the whole race of Adam. The soul of the prophet 'moans for Moab like a lyre',* when, by the agency of sacred scripture, as if in a great harmonious symphony, he instructs the sin-laden soul. He explains how great was the bliss from which it fell and how miserable is the state to which it has come and where it will soon rush in irrevocable ruin, unless the grace of Christ comes to its help.

8. But the words of the preacher are only living and effective* when they produce a deep interior sense of tender compassion and charity, as the prophet goes on to point out. He adds: 'And my heart will sound against the wall of baked brick.'* The 'wall of baked brick' is the soul, hardened now by habits of sin. It is ready to resist the javelins of the fear

of God, the war trumpets of the prophets and the two-edged swords of the preachers, as if its obstinate refusal had surrounded it with a massive palisade. But the heart of the prophet, swelling with tenderness, shatters such a soul, and the great power of the strength of his tears and prayers lays it low. In the end, there is not left in it 'a stone upon a stone, which shall not be destroyed.'*   *Mt 24:2*

This is why the eyes of the church, in so far as regards the office of preaching is concerned, are compared to the pools of Heshbon; they are eyes of watchful vigilance and tender compassion, eyes like pools, for they offer themselves to both good and bad alike, to wash away the stains of sinners.

9. Further, these pools are expressly said to be 'by the gate of the daughter of many',*   *Sg 7:4*
that is, at the entrance gate of the city. This is because the word of the Lord ought to be pressed upon those who enter and depart, and it ought to be pressed upon them vigorously, as the apostle says, in season and out of season.* It was for this reason that   *Cf. 2 Tim 4:2*
Jeremiah was told to stand in the gate of the Lord's house so as to press home his preach-ing.* The result was to make the gate of the   *Cf. Jer 7:2*
Lord's house itself into faithfulness in preach-ing and tender eagerness to listen, or even into the faith of the listeners and the fear of these who obey. Whichever of these you like could well be described as 'the gate of the Lord's house' or 'the gate of the daughter of many'. The mouth of the preacher, through which Christ goes out and enters the soul, hitherto closed to him, is truly a gate of life.

Whoever opens his ear to the word of God, says Christ himself, is already numbered among the blessed.* But faith is also the gateway to life, for through it, life enters into us, and we enter into life, while the psalmist tells us that fear is the beginning of wisdom.*

However, Heshbon is rightly called 'daughter of many', since the city of the repentant, which is what Heshbon means, has an extraordinary large population, a countless throng of citizens. 'See, strangers, and people of Tyre and Ethiopia, these will be her children.'* See, here are all who have been called from pagan lands by grace alone; see, last of all, those who up to now have been ungrateful for grace, who yet sleep in their own filth, and who at last, as at the very last moment of night, will waken up to grace when the morning Sun shines in upon them, saying: 'Arise, be radiant Jerusalem, for your light has come.'* She is indeed 'daughter of many', then, for she gathers into her bosom all the vessels of mercy, and from so countless and varied a throng of citizens, she consecrates, by washing them in her pools, that is, by the sacrament of penance, one single people to the omnipotent God, to the glory and honor of the only Son of the Father,
who, with the same Father and
the Holy Spirit, lives and
reigns, God, for
ever and ever.
Amen.

Cf. Lk 11:28

Cf. Ps 111:10

Ps 87:4

Is 60:1

SERMON SEVENTY-FIVE

The beginning of the seventy-fifth sermon.
How this praise of the bride's eyes can well be
taken as referring to the two kinds of tenderness in the Lord's mother. Of the two kinds of
pools, one which is in Jerusalem for the
cleansing of venial sins, and of the pools in
Heshbon which are said to be for washing of
mortal sins.

'YOUR EYES ARE LIKE pools in
Heshbon, by the gate of the daughter
of many.'*   *Sg 7:4*

If I were to treat of this wedding song and
deprive the Lord's mother of her praise,
especially since that praise shines out more or
less clearly from the mirror which we have in
hand at present, I am afraid that my own
mouth would condemn me. If the whole song
is about her,* in a particular way, would it not   *Cf. Ps 28:7*
be something of a sacrilege not to have given
her even the tiniest part of what is all her
own? Granted that it ill-becomes the tongue
of a sinner to utter what is unutterable to the
mouth of angels and give expression to knowledge which belongs to the saints, all the same,
with her usual condescension she may ap-
prove the stammering efforts of a mouth to
sing her praise, whatever the result may be;
perhaps indeed she may find a place for them

among the high praises that are sounded in heaven. We have no right to think of the most tender mother of Jesus except in the same way that we think about her Son. He made perfect praise for himself from the mouths of infants and suckling babes,* so that the very attempts of infants, and the gestures and desires of those who want to glorify him, become in his mind 'perfect praise'.

2. This verse, therefore, in which the bride's eyes are commanded by her spouse, is concerned with the eyes of the Lord's mother, her own eyes of mercy. Moreover, it so happens that, in a previous part of this poem, her eyes are said to be 'the eyes of doves',* and there the spouse's intention was to praise something else by 'her eyes'. For the dovelike glance of her eyes was meant to honor the sharpness of her spiritual penetration, which keeps her ever gazing, with pure and loving insight, into the face of her spouse and the glory of her Son. But here, in the comparison to the pools of Heshbon, what is praised is the abundance of her tenderness and the gentleness of her regard when she looks at us. Naturally, these most blessed and tranquil eyes hold the happiness of their contemplation utterly without intrusive effort; it is free of anything that would disturb it, it is undistracted by any interruption. With a sublimity completely above that of any other creature, she contemplates 'the Word in the beginning'* and God in man.

3. And in fact, by using the plural form, and saying 'the eyes of doves' instead of 'the eyes of a single dove', it was perhaps intended

that the penetration of that contemplation should be clearly seen as excelling all the other saints who contemplate God's grandeur. Or else it was because the Holy Spirit deigned to appear in the form of a dove,* and he is usually spoken of as 'the sevenfold Spirit', on account of the seven spirits which, according to scripture, have been sent upon the earth.* It would follow that Mary's eyes were described as the eyes of 'doves', since the sevenfold Spirit makes his special abode in her.* In a spiritual sense, this grace is assigned to her eyes, because from the beginning of her very infancy, she consecrated her eyes to the blessed vision of the majesty of God, and disdaining all things of the flesh, she fixed her gaze and focused her attention on the one who absorbed all her affection.

How very greatly the privilege of motherhood added to her virginal purity, and then, the great weight of infinite glory,* that came from the Son of God's taking flesh within her, increased this twofold glory beyond all measure. No human has any inkling of the grace that suffused her loving gaze. It was the gaze of one who contemplated, eye to eye, that great mystery of tender love, a gaze that beheld, face to face, that great brilliancy of light. Even if the human weakness of the child she bore, and her constant knowledge of his baby needs, should have sometimes cast a cloud over her contemplation of his glorious face, the Holy Spirit overshadowed her from that cloud,* and it was from the cloud that the Father of the Lord Jesus thundered the words: 'This is my beloved Son,'* and he is

Cf. Mt 3:16

Cf. Rv 5:6

**Cf. Is 11:2-3.*
Cf. Guerric,
Asspt 1.1; PL 185:
187BC; CF 32:167.

2 Co 4:17

Cf. Lk 1:35

Mt 3:17

your beloved Son, too. Who can tell the story of how, while she contemplated with her constant, dovelike look the Sun of justice, enveloped in her flesh, the sevenfold Spirit irradiated her with his overshadowing, and overshadowed her with his radiance? At one time he gave her the form of wisdom and knowledge, at another he strengthened her with counsel and fortitude: now he enlightened her with knowledge and tender love, now he sealed her with the seal of holy fear, bestowed from heaven.*

4. Those eyes are truly 'the eyes of doves', since, although she knew Christ according to the flesh,* revering him with motherly love according to the flesh assumed from her own self, no one can doubt that she walked 'from brightness into brightness'.* No one can doubt that continual contemplation brought her to a spiritual penetration and that she was translated into that same image.* Paul and men like Paul, may believe that they have attained this, as if it were reflected in the clarity of their words, though somewhat mysteriously. They glory at reaching a point where they are aware of nothing fleshly in Christ,* but, 'beholding the glory of the Lord with unveiled face,'* they say, with him who leaned upon the breast of Jesus,* that they have seen his glory, glory 'as of the only Son of the Father.'* If this is so, it is not much more true than Mary's eyes are 'the eyes of doves', since she is the one on whom the Holy Spirit has poured out all the fullness of his grace?* I say with confidence, that if 'Paul or Apollo or Cephas',* or even the Thrones or

Dominations* or those blessed choirs of spirits inflamed with love,* who cleave to God without intermediary, if any of these should direct the gaze of their heart as keenly as possible, they would still be darkness in comparison with those 'eyes of doves'.

If each one walks, as the apostle says, from glory into glory,* not of his own power but in the Spirit of the Lord, surely a greater infusion of the Spirit will mean a more total surrender of the heart to God? In a unique way, then, for her who loves God above all rational spirits, there is this particular and continual cry to the Father of spirits: 'My soul faints for your salvation, and I have trusted in your word: my eyes have failed with watching for your promise.'* My soul faints, because of the vehement longing of love; my eyes faint, through the tireless zeal of my understanding. Where there is love, there is the eye, too, and the soul fainting away with holy love attributes its exhaustion from this faintness to the eyes.

5. Notice that there are three causes of this exhaustion, or, to put it more plainly, three subjects that incite to love: salvation, God's word, God's promise.* Every loving soul rightly faints for salvation, since it was through the mystery of the incarnation and passion that salvation came to us. God's word, on the other hand, incites us because there Christ revealed himself unmistakably as the only Son of God, equal to the Father. And we faint for his promise because whatever he has heard from the Father, he has made known to us,* and he has written it on

Col 1:16

The Seraphim

Cf. 2 Co 3:18

Ps 119:81-82

Cf. Jn 1:1

Jn 15:15

Cf. 2 Co 3:2

Cf. Jn 5:19

our hearts through the Holy Spirit.* The salvation of God is the Lord Jesus, who achieved our salvation in his own person; in the word of God, and everything that the Father does, Christ himself does the same things, in the same way;* he is the promise of God, not only declaring the message of life to the mind, but also promising it to the heart as something already effective. It is very understandable that this soul and these eyes should be occupied all day long with their concern for things like these.

Of course, even if it is not able to grasp these mysteries fully, however much it concentrates, the endeavors of the fainting soul, or the faintness of the endeavoring soul are not for that reason ever rendered fruitless and in vain. Nothing in the whole of life can be thought of that is more useful than faintings of this kind, and there is nothing that conduces more to spiritual health than these weaknesses.

Ps 36:9

But the sweetest and most tranquil way of looking, one that we find very wonderful, is that of the virgin mother. She fainted for the Lord Jesus, in fact, still faints to this day, if we may say this of her, and of those blessed spirits who 'see the light in the light'.* Just as they still hunger and thirst, so do they still faint. Let us turn our attention to those eyes in the same way as they are intent on us. If we think along these lines, then, the virgin mother's eyes are compassion and mercy. They are compassion, in that she compassionates sinners: they are mercy, in that she implores repentance and forgiveness for them.

Their pity is infinite, because she keeps men
back from sin by following the example of
her Son.* Their mercy, too, is very rich,
because she supports sinners and listens to
their prayers. On one hand, she calls back
those who have turned away from God, and
draws back those who are for the most part
ignorant and unwilling. But on the other
hand, she tenderly escorts those who have
already returned, and hastens to reconcile
the suppliants to God. This is why those eyes
are deservedly likened to pools, in which dirt
can usually be washed away.

6. But notice that there is one pool in
Jerusalem, and another in Heshbon. We have
the evidence of the evangelist that there is a
pool in Jerusalem, called *probatica* and containing five porches, and that in the past, 'a
great crowd of the sick lay there, waiting for
the moving of the water.'* Then the gospel
adds, that 'the angel of the Lord came down
at certain times into the pool, and the waters
were moved,'* and whoever first entered them
after this, was healed.* This pool is called
probatica, after *probaton,* which is a name
for sheep, as a result of its having been
consecrated for the washing of sheep for
sacrifice. Let us see if the reason why
the spouse only makes mention of the pools
in Heshbon, in contradistinction to this pool,
which is in Jerusalem, set aside for sheep,
may not be precisely because of the sheep.
Just as one pool is for sheep, so the other
pool is for goats. Clearly, both flocks require
washing, if they are to be made into a sacrifice, but sheep need a little washing, and

*Cf. Bernard,
O Asspt 2;
SBOp 5:263.*

Jn 5:1-3

Jn 5:4

Jn 5:3

goats a great deal.

The Jerusalem pool is described as having five porches, on account of the five separate senses which are each restrained from worldly allurements. The Heshbon pools, though, are said to be 'by the gate of the daughter of many,'* that is, full in the fear of God's punishments. In fact, the gates of Heshbon are quite different from the gates of the daughter of Zion. At the gates of Heshbon, there is confession of great sins; at the gates of the daughter of Zion, there is also confession, but of venial sins, followed by praise of God. 'Enter his gates', says the psalm, 'with confession, his courts with hymns of praise.'* So the gates of the daughter of Zion are characterized by the twofold confession of sins and of praise, but the gate of Heshbon, or the daughter of many, is only a single gate, from its one single and simple type of confession.

At times, the angel of the Lord came down into the sheep pool*, because, as we have shown, those who come often to its saving font, by their two kinds of confession, are visited with angelic consolation more often. Obviously, all the sick, who long for healing, wait eagerly for the descent of the angel, for if anyone were too careless in watching, he might be deprived of the sight of the angel and of his own salvation.

7. We are the ones, dearest brothers, we are the ones whom this parable concerns. Never may sleep take us by surprise, when the angel is coming down; never let us be found careless and uninterested in plunging

Sg 7:4

Ps 100:4

Cf. Jn 5:2

ourselves into that saving font, when the waters of the pool are stirred. In all earnestness, when we behold the water moving, when the thoughts of our heart are roused to compunction, it is the Lord's angel, the grace of our redeemer, flashing from heaven. But if we do not go out to meet the coming angel, if we do not receive with great haste the gift of grace that is offered, another man comes before us, and gets our blessing first.*   *Cf. Jn 5:7* When the grace offered us, is spurned, it is certainly bestowed on somebody more eager, to whom it had not yet been offered. Once the word of heavenly grace has left the mouth of the Most High, it cannot return to him empty,* but if it is ungraciously repelled, it   *Cf. Is 55:11* gives blessing to new sons of grace.

But 'the Man who is called Jesus',* can   *Jn 9:11* also heal this ingratitude and the illness of sloth, especially when the invalid humbly confesses how idle his disease makes him, and does not rely on his own strength, abandoning himself wholly to him who alone is strong. 'While I am coming,' he says, 'another goes ahead of me, because I have nobody to put me into the pool when the water is moved.'* Here is a humble con-   *Jn 4:7* fession of a penitent's weakness, and here is the high priest to hear it. All that remains is for the priest to forgive the penitent and absolve him for his confession. O man, now the angel has truly moved the water for you! Now at length you do have somebody to put you in the pool, after the waters are moved! Now he plunges you right in, and you are baptized anew, and emerging at long last from your habitual weakness, you will never again suffer the captivity of a bed of idleness. In fact, he who made you whole, made you so whole that he can say: 'Arise, take up your bed, and walk.'*

Indeed, it has been in vain, and quite useless, for you to rise before dawn,* since it was highly presumptuous to attempt anything, however small, without the help of grace. But now grace has shone upon you, and it is no longer foolish to rise before dawn and call to God, your helper: 'God, my God, to you do I watch at dawn.'* This means: God, my God, it is by the light of your grace, that I watch for you. Consequently, to prove that you are completely cured, 'take up your bed and walk.'* Never should so great a grace slip from your memory, that you have escaped from so great an illness. 'Take up your bed,'* extolling Christ who has visited you, and confessing now with praise what you have just confessed with repentance. 'Take up your bed,'* so that your sickness will no more lord it over you, but you will be lord of it. It may weigh you down, but it can no longer imprison you, and if it presses, at least it does not oppress you any more. In future, it will be for you a sign of health, not a hindrance to virtue.

8. So it is not said: in Jerusalem, that is, in the assembly of the saints, there is the pool of *probatica,* which an angel from heaven visits, and which the Lord Jesus visits even more often, to heal the sick. No, very strangely, what is referred to in this love song, are the pools of Heshbon. Heshbon

lies outside the borders of Judea, in the land of Moab, which, according to Isaiah, is so 'very proud that its pride and arrogance is greater than its fortitude.'* Let me stress this: it is to these Moabite pools that the bride's eyes are compared by her spouse. But what wonder if there are words that amaze us, when there are deeds far more amazing! For those eyes of the mother of mercy, eyes most gentle, gaze, not only upon the careless and idle in the church, but even upon the shameless and those who are still wrapped up in their filth. Could we not call them 'Moabites', those who take their being from Moab, begotten of an incestuous marriage, that is, marriage with a father? And they are very much their father's children, not only in race, but in likeness, being themselves drunken and incestuous. Will it not be altogether necessary to have a pool of many waters to wash away this kind of filth?

Indeed, why should the virgin mother come to the gate of Heshbon, except because of the greatness of her tenderness? She tells us: 'I shall make you drunk with my tears, Heshbon and Elealeh.'* But we cannot mistake whose voice it is; it is the tender voice of Jesus speaking to sinners. In all truth, it is the message of Jesus, who once saw a somewhat similar city, 'and wept over it, saying: If only you had known!'* Yes, it is Jesus who speaks to those who pass by the way, and asks them to see 'if there is any sorrow like this.'* Yes, there are no tears like the tears of Jesus, no sorrow like the sorrow of Jesus. His sorrow breaks open the hardened

Is 16:5

Is 16:9

Lk 19:42

Lm 1:12

Cf. Is 16:1

Cf. Rm 8:29

Is 16:9

Cf. Ps 69:4

Sg 7:4

heart of the sinner, and he repents. His tears draw a spring of tears from the rock of the desert.* It is truly impossible for any soul not to be pierced sooner or later to contrition, and it was for this that Jesus shed tears. It is an established fact that Jesus grieved and wept, and over and above, offered his own self as a victim of reparation to his eternal Father, for all those whom he foreknew and predestined to be restored through penance.*

9. So this is the loving lament of ancient compassion and eternal predestination: 'I shall make you drunk with my tears, Heshbon and Elealeh.'* It is as if he lamented from the depths of his heart, speaking to the throng of sinners who would be justified by the sacrament of penance. It is as if he says: I restore on your account what you have stolen;* I do penance first, for your sins. You too, will be sorry, but it will be because of the tears of my penance rather than because of your tears, that you will be justified. If you too are to feel contrition, my tears will have to be your drink; if you are to do real penance, my tears will have to make you drunk.

The pools of Heshbon, then, are the deep compassion of God, which made him do penance for sinners in the past, and the unfettered, secret inspiration of all repentance. It is right that these pools should be said to stand 'by the gate of the daughters of the many,'* because they come before all merit, and all the beginning of holiness is within them, and because they present themselves, day and night, to those who are going out of their old and evil house to be cleansed. Or it could be because 'by the gate' means the Lord Jesus, since only with him is mercy, 'and fullness of redemption.'*

Ps 130:7

10. So it is to these pools that the eyes of the bride, who is the Lord's mother, are compared with most delicate praise. In fact, I say with confidence, that not even the spouse could find anything in all his house and store to which he could more nobly liken those eyes of hers. This is why the whole church of the saints, too, as if taking over the word, calls her 'mother of mercy'. Like eternal Mercy Itself, she anticipates and comes to help, she runs before and comes to greet, she sees from far off and she looks close from near at hand.*

Cf. Eph 2:17

And now, O tenderest of mothers, 'look on the face of your Christ,'* and hasten to turn on us, too, those merciful eyes of yours, after looking on the tender face of your Son.* Remember, I beg you, the children of Zion, and recall as well, the children of Heshbon. Be mindful of those who call on your name from the bosom of the church, and be mindful too, of Rahab and Babylon,* who know you through the name and glory of your blessed Son, who, with God the Father
and the Holy Spirit, lives and reigns,
God, for ever and ever.
Amen.

Ps 84:9

*Cf. Antiphon,
Salve Regina.*

Cf. Ps 87:4

The beginning of the seventy-sixth sermon.
Of the persecution of the Cistercians in England,* and of the ardor of some who are more eager for worldly freedom than is just.

See C. J. Holdsworth, 'John of Ford and the Interdict'; EHR 78 (1963) 705-14.

'YOUR NOSE IS LIKE the tower of Lebanon, which looks towards Damascus.'*

Sg 7:4

In his great generosity, the spouse presses on loyally with the task he has undertaken, and makes superb acknowledgement of his beloved in the presence of his Father and the daughters of Jerusalem, that is, the holy angels and spirits of the blessed,* whom he thinks deserve to hear this marriage hymn. Happy is the soul whom the Holy Spirit admits into this audience, who has the privilege of experiencing even the smallest fragment of that marriage joy, provided it can hold what it lays hold of.

Cf. Mt 10:32

But what has this song to do with us? We have been given over to be plundered,* and we expect nothing any more except ruin and destruction. It is necessary to confess this very clearly, since this is an occasion, when, as is his custom, the Lord Jesus has come in 'to look at those who sit at table.'* And this is a tragedy for us in our beggarly poverty, because he finds us without a wedding garment.* The gaiety of a bridegroom has changed into the

Cf. Tob 3:4

Mt 22:11

Ibid.

sterness of a judge; he has overturned the tables, he has thrown the guests into confusion, and by a new and terrifying miracle, he has made the wine become water.* O loving Jesus, why have you treated us like this?* Are you truly making ready to blot us out from your sight? Are you preparing to do away with 'the portion of your own inheritance',* which up to now has been to the glory of your name? We wait in suspense, and this is like a swollen ulcer, still supporting and not yet covered with a healing scar.* Look at us, listening to one thing after another, wounded by blow upon blow. Unless you yourself come in haste to heal us, sudden death is imminent.

2. The parable is very clear, and no one who will take the trouble to read or listen to these things will have any difficulty in understanding it. But, 'so that the next generation may understand, and that the children yet to be born,' the children of the saints, 'may arise and tell their children,'* and their children's children, I shall speak in plain language. I shall speak without any imagery or parable of what everyone today is fully conscious. For look at what has happened: from the king's presence there has suddenly issued a decree* that puts all the property of our houses into the hands of despoilers. Sheep and cattle and all other animals, as well as all the wheat that the labor of the reapers had only recently stored in the barns: everything is hurriedly disposed of, at the command of the royal decree. Cattle pens stand empty and so do the barns. Everything that had been painfully and laboriously

gathered together for many years back for the support of the poor, has been broken into, laid bare, squandered, without any scruple or reverence for God's name. In fact, this edict of the king's has urged those in the vicinity not to be dilatory in purchasing. For many, fear of public power outweighed their respect for God, and for the most part, they came forth to swallow us up as if to ceremonial spoils. For it must not be called a biting, but a real 'swallowing up', when, wholly without pity, the inexorable and quite insatiable fury of our enemies, opened its jaws in an infinite gape, like the fury of hell. Their intention was to swallow down everything.

3. Need I continue? In this distress, there was nothing left but to go humbly to the king and, on our knees, like dutiful children, implore him to modify his rage and show us mercy. Moreover, the sole reason for this rage was that when the king was about to set out for Ireland with the army, and the abbots were summoned with regard to the raising of money, they rejected his request. They were terrified that the privilege, which this order has been accustomed to enjoy from ancient times, was going to be encroached upon, and they begged to have their freedom from taxation preserved inviolate, as in the past. They implored the king at least to wait until they could receive an answer to this problem from their general chapter. At this reply, the wrath of the king blazed up like fire, and there is no doubt at all that it was on that day that he conceived the plan that we now realize has

been brought to birth in the groans of us all. For a few days, while he lingered in Ireland, our trial held fire, but all the time, the fear of his coming judgement and a sort of terrible sense of expecting a sentence, made our hearts very anxious.

And now, undisguised, 'the fear that I feared came upon me, and what I dreaded, befell me.'* The royal verdict was that there was no alternative left except for us to do exactly what he demanded, or else we would all have to take farewell of our monasteries. But where was all this mass of men to go? Certainly, if the sheep were to be scattered,* the wolf would be constantly slavering after them, drawing them back into the past entanglements of their former sins, or to even worse. Surely, good shepherds had to take precautions against this, and, if need arose, were bound to lay down their lives for the good of their flock.* How much more, then, were they indifferent to the fear of having their possessions squandered.

But there were some who saw the matter differently. They chose to retire and withdraw, rather than to put into the moneybags of the sacrilegious the goods of the poor, the wealth bestowed by God and what men call 'the patrimony of the crucified Christ'. They hold it is better to let these men seize whatever they please, rather than become themselves collaborators with thieves and agents in these acts of plunder. In general, their position was a refusal to carry the immensity of the imposed levy, preferring not to take up the burden at all rather than bear its weight.

Jb 3:25

Cf. Mk 14:27

Cf. Jn 11:11

But for most of them, as I have said, the first consideration was the salvation of souls, and hence they devoted themselves to dealing with this disastrous financial loss, and it did not seem to them that this served the cause of wickedness. They followed the gospel precept to 'give place to anger',* in all humility, in case, by resisting authority, they might deserve the apostle's accusation of 'resisting God'.* They decided, finally, that those who were overtaken by a furious storm must use their discretion. To their way of thinking, men must lighten the ship when, on all sides, towering waves threaten to drown them, and no image dwells before their eyes but that of pallid death. However precious the treasure they jettison, they regard it as a trifle in comparison with their own safety. The wise merchant will not hesitate to give all he has, for the sake of his soul.*

So then, if the price of temporal safety and of drawing breath for a little while is so high, that nothing this world holds dear can possibly be compared to it, how much more careful we should be about the value of souls, which Christ died to redeem, and of a safety that is not passing but eternal? This is especially so for those souls who, as the gospel promises, a very strict accounting must be made.*

4. Moreover, we know that 'the disciple is not above his master,'* and it ought to satisfy all our expectations, or even go beyond them, if we live in these present times with a freedom as great as our Master's. And in fact, it was in the Master's mouth, he who

Cf. Rm 12:19

Rm 13:2

Cf. Mt 13:46

Cf. Heb 13:17

Mt 10:24

is Lord of all freedom, that Peter found the
coin, and the whole church with him.* Jesus
is the first among the fish, since he is 'the
firstborn from the dead',† and he is 'the first
and only free man among mortals.'* In him,
the prince of this world has found nothing
that is his,* and no earthly king, since he
possesses no thing of this earth, has the right
to make on him any demands.* So Simon
Peter fished for this Prince of true freedom,
concealed in the great sea of our salty water.
He fished with the hook of faith and love for
this Fish who knows nothing of sea's salt,
and gave him to the church to be eaten.

Then to his amazement, when he opened
the mouth of this holy Fish, he found in it a
coin.* At that time, it was a cause of great
wonder that from the mouth of the eternal
Caesar there had gone forth a decree so
binding that he did not refuse to have himself
and all his church enrolled.* His order was for
them both to meet the demands of the en-
rollers. 'Let the earth hear, and all its richness,'* let the heavens hear and all who dwell
in them, that in the mouth of Him who is
'King of kings and Lord of lords,'* a coin has
been found. He who is wholly without 'the
image and inscription of Caesar'*, takes the
service of Caesar upon himself, and does so
incontrovertibly. And a servitude of this kind
is not only no hindrance to true freedom, but
serves and advances it. 'You were called as a
slave; never mind. But if you have a chance to
be free, take it.'* This is the apostle's advice.

Some people have thought that this remark
of St Paul's should be understood in a more

Cf. Mt 17:26,
Anselm of Laon,
Enar. in Matt. *18;*
PL 162:1405BC.
†Cf. Col 1:18
*Ps 88:5.

Cf. Jn 14:30

Cf. Mt 17:26

Mt 17:27

Ibid.

Is 34:1

Rv 19:16

Mt 22:20

1 Co 7:21

profound sense, which has him apparently preferring slavery to freedom, as if his real meaning were: if you have a chance to be free, take slavery in preference. For just as 'suffering produces endurance',* and is in fact the tutor of endurance, and as fear is the fashioner of charity,* though the fashioning tool may be the hammer of penance, so it is with slavery. Servitude in this world leads humbly and profitably to that true and heavenly freedom which is humility and meekness. Any of us, then, who is zealous for that true freedom, which is in Christ, if we are truly experienced in the things of Christ, if we faithfully taste and savor the Fish who was the first to come up from the sea and do all we can to come out of the sea with him, with Christ, then we must not let the bitterness of suffering overwhelm us. We must not let the salt endanger us. We must see and look very carefully, not at what lies hidden in the closed mouth of the Fish, but at what now lies exposed.

5. For this time, the Wisdom of God did not speak in parables as he usually did.* Without any mystery, by both word and deed, he enrolled himself and Peter, and in Peter the universal church, in the school of this most humble way of life. Further, the author of all ages, chose especially to be born in that particular age when the whole earth was enrolled by its territorial lord.* He came down from heaven to his own,* and he claimed nothing in the world for his personal use except swaddling bands and a manger. So he was immediately reckoned as no more important than any other man; their lot was

slavery, and he never shrank from entering upon it. And it was then, indeed, that from this vast sea of Adam's race, the first free man of the sons of Adam came up alone out of the sea, and in his mouth, though it was still closed, there was yet found a coin.* Yes, it was closed, but only while the Word was silent. Yet even then it was already opened by the significance of his action and, as it seems to us, by his acceptance of slavery.

6. But if Jesus appeared to speak in parables up to this time, he 'opened his mouth' when he forestalled the question Peter was about to put to him, and 'asked him: From who do the kings of the earth accept tribute, from their sons or from strangers?'* When Peter answered: 'From strangers,'* Jesus at once concluded: 'Then the sons are free! However, not to give offense to them, go to the sea and cast a hook, and take the first fish that comes up. When you open its mouth you will find a coin. Take that and give it to them for me and for yourself.'*

What could be more open? Yes, now he is speaking clearly, and he uses no figure of speech.* Indeed, if he had ordered the tax to be paid only for himself, he would have left room for our anxious subtlety to discuss the matter, as well as playing into the hands of the disciple's worldliness. They were always eager for the same things as the pharisees, and he would not have cut away this worldly desire of theirs for freedom, since he could well have been thought to have paid only this one tax in such a way as to thereby redeem Peter, and in him, the whole church, from ever again having a levy imposed upon them. Consequently, in his wisdom, he suckled his worldly disciples by opening his mouth, and taught them about liberty of the Spirit, laying it down that the cost of this passing slavery was to be paid for himself together with Peter, that is, for himself and the church.

Take the time when the Jews were still confused by the greatness of his light, and were not able, under the influence of so great an example, to produce anything of spiritual value. When the master of truth was interrupted and asked about this question, he had no hesitation in opening his mouth still wider. What he said was: 'Render to Caesar the things that are Caesar's, and to God the things that are God's.'* So, even when he was being tested by hypocrites, he opened his mouth to reveal, even then, a coin. Better, the coin was not just found there, it was explicitly revealed. For, however widely Jesus opened his mouth, when he was surrounded by hypocrites who planned merely to ask trick questions, there could not be 'found' any perception of this true and mysterious freedom. 'The unspiritual man does not perceive the things of God's Spirit.'*

7. In fact, to this day, even for many who are thoroughly well grounded in christian doctrines, this statement about slavery of this kind is a very disputed point; I could almost say they consider it 'folly'.* Right up to now, whether it is the mouth of Christ that opened, or the mouth of Paul that lies wide, their mouths are considered as shut. Obviously, these men must be afraid of

assuming the superstitious zeal of the pharisees, of having a justice that is not so much true as hypocritical. In other words, they fear obeying the commands of kings in case they find themselves becoming agents in an unjust taxation and thereby involved in equal guilt with them.

The man who seeks the perfection of the gospels offers his other cheek to whoever strikes it,* and when forced to go one mile, decides that he must go another two as well with his tormentor.* Will a man like this be thought of as assenting to violence and force? Will he not be seen as a disciple of the Truth and the best follower of the gospel? The Lord Jesus, too: when an unjust demand was made, did he do wrong in acceding to it? Was his payment not rather deeply just, because deeply humble, and deeply righteous because deeply worthy of himself? Did he not embrace with arms of welcome the cross that was laid upon him, though the verdict was most evil and unjust? He was not ashamed to bear this burden on his willing shoulders, and can he then be thought of as having collaborated with the sentence of wicked men? Surely he appears rather as the agent of the will of God and the teacher of all patience and humility. He did not take his chalice from the hand of Pilate or from the hand of the Jews, 'the hands of iniquity'.* No, he accepted it eagerly as offered to him by his Father,* and he gladly drained it.

And the fortitude, too, that shone out so brightly in holy Job, after he had lost so much of his property, and so often: where did it

Ct. Mt 5:39

Mt 5:41

Ps 144:8
Cf. Mt 26:39

come from, if not from his belief that it was the Lord, and not the devil who had taken it all away? This was why he put his hand over his mouth and cursed the day of his birth,* but he did not curse those who plundered his possessions, nor did he curse (which God forbid), God's decree. David also, who was 'a man after God's own heart',* had very little to say when he was overwhelmed by persecution. He bore it patiently because God sent it, and humbly did not retaliate against the human agents. This is why, when the saints who form this mighty army die, their death is precious,* and there rises that splendid and triumphal cry: 'I will take the chalice of salvation, and call upon the name of the Lord.'* So if we too are truly of this noble breed, should not the same dispositions clothe us? Should not the same freedom give us the strength to refer all the persecution we now suffer to God, the judge of all, the first cause of all, that is, eternal justice? We assent to what has happened, if this is what pleases the Lord, and we prepare our hearts to offer the other cheek to the striker.*

8. But let these words suffice for the moment. Let us now continue with a few things that were actually carried out against us at court. I will use myself as an example, to make it clear in what case others also stood. When I pleaded with the king for our abbey, all I earned from his mouth was abuse, and as God is my witness, I accepted it as if it spoke from heaven—or rather, thundered. For it came like a thunderclap. When I put forward the excuse of our poverty, the king

retorted: 'A fat monk is no good to anyone!' And by 'fat', he meant to imply 'rich'. The king added: 'When he is fat, he never hesitates to make false accusations against his neighbors, he takes possession of his neighbors' lands, he gets hold of other people's heritage, he disturbs and wrongs everybody else, he devotes himself to arranging profitable marriage for his relatives. But the thin monk has at last begun to be a good member of society, one who fits in with his neighbors and superiors.'

So it was violent reproaches like this that were heaped upon me when I pressed on with my very humble petitions, pointing out that our abbey had not the means to take on so very great a burden: it was seven hundred and fifteen marks that he had demanded. But I achieved absolutely nothing. Nothing, I repeat, was of any use to me, and that I knew by experience, since for a period of three years I had been the king's confessor and almsgiver, an arrangement made by Archbishop Hubert of blessed memory, of the see of Canterbury.‡ When I realized that I was doing nothing as confessor, I withdrew from the office, by God's mercy, and in my place was appointed my brother abbot of Bindon.‡‡

‡ Hubert Walter (1193–1205), dean of York, bishop of Salisbury, and companion of Richard the Lion-hearted on crusade before being elevated to the See of Canterbury. For a time he was simultaneously archbishop, royal justiciar, and papal legate. For a contemporary account of his energetic activities, and edifying death, see Ralph Coggeshall, *Chronicon anglicanum* (Roll Series).
‡‡ Henry of Bindon. Henry had succeeded John as abbot of Bindon in Dorset, a daughter house of Ford, when John turned to Ford to accept the abbacy in 1191. Henry also resigned, in 1212, to become bishop of Emly, in Ireland. He died in 1227.

His experience was the same as mine: in the beginning, he seemed to be achieving something there, but as time went on, it was little or nothing.

9. So, as I have said, I left the king's presence, weighed down by the sheer size of so great a burden, and unable to lessen this huge sum in the slightest, no matter how earnestly I pleaded. I could not even gain the respite of a single day. Yet the period of time allowed us was very short, that is, no more than six weeks to pay half this sum, and the other half before the end of five weeks. The exceedingly short time we were given forced us to sell our possessions for practically nothing, especially since the king had told one of my fellow abbots, among other things, that to be one day late would cost him a hundred marks. And so without more ado, there was a great selling: oxen, who but yesterday were pulling the plough, were released from the yoke, and cows, with calves and heifers, sheep too, and any other animals we had, estates and rents, even the very clothes the community had to wear, not to mention our very food, our books as well, and our sacred vessels, all, all were sold.

Just as in a sudden outbreak of fire, or in the terror of a shipwreck, so it was now. Everyone pressed on to search out and dispose of all our property, doing all they could to help with might and main the work of saving the community. In the end, by God's mercy, we were rescued from the impending shipwreck, but—or so we fear—only to have sold into perpetual slavery and brought into disrepute all around us. We have begun to walk a new road of poverty, also, and this means we no longer have the strength to lift our heads in public.

But does this really matter? O, if only, at long last, this enforced servitude would bring us back even a little, in God's sight, to genuine poverty! We had gone very far away from it, fugitives and exiles. Now that this blow has fallen, may the bottomless abyss of this greed come at last to an end.

10. Indeed, speaking about this, I remember a vision I heard of, unforgettable but very terrible. When our abbots were on their way to Northampton, where it had been arranged that they would reply to the king about this problem, one of them, a deeply religious man, saw in a dream the Lord Jesus, hanging from the wood of the cross and surrounded by abbots and monks. He hung from his cross, right enough, but the nails had been taken out and he was not fixed to it in the usual way. No, he was weakly attached by the soft lines that women wear. Everyone called upon him, loudly and repeatedly, while he hung his head and made no response to their cries, and remained unmoved. But they went on crying out, and he finally raised himself, displeased. He spoke to them as if he were in labor pangs, and what he said was: A curse upon your day! These words were a thunderbolt, waking the visionary from his trance. He gave himself up to tears and lamentations, and to this very day, no one has been able to allay his grief completely.

11. But what this vision means is clear

enough. We have only to refer it to the opinions of the abbots themselves and to the true state of affairs. Christ appeared like this, since this actually is how we do treat him in this wretched life of ours. It is by nails of poverty and mortification, yes, and by nails of fear and love that he must be fixed to his cross in our lives. But we have drawn out those nails, by a pretense of gentleness and tenderness, and by taking care to serve him by observances motivated more by dry custom than by living faith. Living like this, these womanly hearts, set on a female softness, do not have Christ crucified with them, because they themselves are not nailed with Christ to the cross.* So, since he is certainly not roused by the cries of those whom he does not in any way consider friends of his cross, he cannot bless them when he wakes.

On the contrary, he curses their day, meaning by that, their peace, their complacency, their life of pleasure, their prosperity. In short, he is cursing this liberty of ours, in which we have been accustomed to take so much boastful comfort. This has certainly been a source of pride for us, more than for any of the church's sons, and it continues to this very day, coming both from the patronage of the popes and from the singular favor shown by our kings. And it is equally certain that this special position has made us vain and conceited. We may deny it, but 'God has found out the sinful ways of his servants.'* What we heard a little while ago from the prophet Ezekiel, has happened to us. He saw this vine of ours, which the right hand of the Lord had taken out of Egypt and planted, carefully and at cost.* Yes, just as it is written there, he saw its height with the great mass of its branches,* and while he looked, it was suddenly rooted up in wrath.* So, on this day, the crucified Christ cursed this day of ours, using the same harsh curse that he used through the lips of holy Job, when he cursed his day.* But Christ changed Job's curse into a rich blessing, and it is my hope that he did not give us this answer from the cross to destroy us, but rather to rebuke.

And now, Lord Jesus, in accordance with what you said, may that day perish, the day on which we strive either to find or to live in worldly content, right up to the present, and may our soul die your death, the death of your cross. May a new day dawn for us, a day of your holy poverty and your holy love, may the truth of your cross be restored, so that, on whatever day we call upon you, you will not turn away your ear, you will not cover your face,* but you will listen to us without delay. Then you will bless us, you who, with God, the Father and the Holy Spirit,
are blessed above all that is,
God forever and ever.
Amen.

The beginning of the seventy-seventh sermon.
Of the Bride's nose, and how to praise it is to
praise either the strength of her discretion or
the keenness of her power of scent. This is the
power that usually enables her through the
acuteness of interior devotion, to track down
and follow her spouse.

'YOUR NOSE IS LIKE the tower of Lebanon, which looks towards Damascus.'*

For some days, now, we have been silent in the presence of the wicked, who made us suffer unbearably. Yet we should rather say: in the Lord's presence, since 'at the presence of the Lord, the earth was moved,'* but not at their presence. We should thank God that it was not without reason, and not without rich fruit, that this storm hung over us and the sea rose in such violent surges. I feel that it all made my heart a good deal humbler, and that repeated appeals to the name of Jesus made the mountains and hills of my towering pride bow low and subside,* moving them far into the heart of the sea. Through your strength, Lord, and through the force of your anger, this has come about in all the houses of our order throughout the country, and I pray that your controlling providence will see to it that

Sg 7:4

Ps 114:7

Cf. Is 40:4
Cf. Mt 18:6

the mountains which bent down in your presence, never again increase and rise afresh.

O Guide of the humble, you have shattered the two horns of our forehead, which made our order seem pre-eminent in the eyes of men.* I am referring to the privilege of a twofold exemption, loftier than anybody else's, that lay in aristocratic ease beneath the shadow of kings and popes. See what has happened: at your rebuke, that shadow disappeared, or, far more truly, in your compassion the denser shadow of your protection appeared, the shadow of your wings,* the column of cloud,* a sure stay of refuge. May those who flee to it be ready to say: The Spirit before our face is Christ the Lord, and 'under his shadow we shall live among the nations.'*

And now, Lord, we have thrown ourselves upon you: do not reject us! We look only towards you, do not, please, despise us! For truly, 'the Egyptian is a man, not a god, and their horses are flesh, not spirit.'* 'Truly, the hills are a delusion, and the orgies on the mountains,'* to which in vain we used to lift up our eyes.* But now it is you who must be 'our army every morning, and our salvation in the time of this trouble,'* seeing that it is in the greatness of your strong arm that we may pass unharmed through this sea, dry shod.* And night too shall have its song, as scripture says, 'Who gives songs in the night.'* Otherwise, how will we fulfill the words, 'I shall bless the Lord at all times,'* if night imposes a perpetual silence? So, after his words of rebuke, which he spoke as judge, when we

Cf. Ex 34:30

Ps 17:8
Ex 13:21

Lm 4:20

Is 31:3

Jr 3:24
Cf. Ps 121:1

Is 33:2

Cf. Ex 15:16

Jb 35:10

Ps 34:1

 John of Ford

Cf. Lm 1:19

were on trial before him during this affliction, I gladly return to his words of affection, which revive the contrite spirit.*

2. He takes up again the praises of his bride, then, speaking before the maidens, and he speaks of his bride and to her. 'Your nose is like the tower of Lebanon, which looks towards Damascus.'* The nose, as our teachers rightly think,* symbolizes the virtue of discretion, and if this is so, it comes fittingly towards the end, when many of the bride's virtues have already been discussed and commended. Discretion is for her the governor and tutor of all the other virtues. Obviously, this is why the skilful precautions against lurking evils, as well provide a strong defense when they come out into the open.

In fact, it is the special quality of discretion to hold in suspicion those vices which attack all the more dangerously because of their appearance of virtue, and to make our fellow men suspect them also. Examples would be: false piety, too extreme an austerity, an over-free merriment, an uncontrolled severity, and, something we see seeping through the whole body of the church at present, a powerful and fierce desire for worldly freedom. This is the very thing which, in the former kingdom of the Jews, furnished the occasion for their overthrow. They raised their necks on high, struggling to throw off the yoke of slavery imposed upon them. They refused to pay tribute, and so became captives of the sword. They were thrust into perpetual slavery, after their short-lived freedom. The apostle warned

Sg 7:4

*Cf. Gregory the Great, Moralia 31.44.85; PL 76:619D-20A.

them. 'Pay all men their dues: taxes to whom taxes are due, tribute to whom tribute is due, respect to whom respect is due, honor to whom honor is due,'* but they refused to heed him. So in the end they were forced to hear the prophet, who drove them away and cast them out.* Go, he says, 'those who are for pestilence, to pestilence, and those who are for the sword, to the sword; those who are for famine, to famine, and those who are for captivity, to captivity.'*

When the time came, then, for the spouse to tell his former bride, repudiated Israel, that her nakedness was to be exposed to the gaze of her lovers,* he also threatened that her nose would be cut off.* Since she took no notice of God's justice, and kept submitting all her doings to the eyes of men, covering them with what one might call hypocritical activity, her power to discern justice was taken away from her, by God's just decree. As a result, her foulness was laid bare for all to see, and her shameful folly.

3. This is the reason for Israel's passionate and unquenchable thirst for christian blood, as if she had erected a tower for herself in Damascus, directly opposite the new Jerusalem. The meaning of 'Damascus', of course, is 'drink of blood',* indicating that long-standing envy of the synagogue, eaten up with desire for the church's joys, unknown to her. It was to Damascus, as to a great fortified tower, that Paul was hastening, in those days when he breathed out threats and slaughter.* But when he entered Damascus, he had been changed instantaneously from wolf into lamb,

Rm 13:7

Cf. Jr 15:1

Jr 15:2

Cf. Ezk 16:37
Cf. Ezk 23:25

Jerome, Liber de nom. heb.; *PL 23: 847, 853; CC 72: 64, 145.*

Cf. Ac 9:1

Cf. Ac 9:4

after the Lamb looked at him from heaven.* So he consecrated the tower of Damascus as the tower of Lebanon, and reverently drank the blood of the Lamb which he had previously thirsted after so irreverently. The thirst he had was certainly changed, but it was not in the least suffocated or diminished. Who can be unaware that Paul thirsted for the blood of many, and drank it, too? He never ceased drawing and urging men to martyrdom with just as much urgency as he had once drawn them savagely and cruelly to prison.* Surely these are the words of one thirsting for blood: 'The sufferings of this present time are not worthy to be compared with the glory that will be revealed in us'?* And again, when he says that he glories in the cross of our Lord Jesus Christ,* and tells everybody that they should glory in it, this can only mean that he is athirst for everyone's blood.

Cf. Ac 9:13

Rm 8:18

Cf. Gal 6:14

4. Damascus, then, indicates the false justice of the synagogue, and the false freedom she has erected in opposition to the name of christian. However, it also symbolizes the appearance of truth and freedom by which the church mantles and screens herself, at least in respect to her external worship. Her aim here is not to please her heavenly spouse, but rather the eyes of her lovers, into whose arms she madly throws herself. Indeed, as far as pertains to the serious use of the smell, she is shown as having a beautiful and prominent nose. If you look only at the keenness of her discernment, she never ceases, day or night, to exercise her senses in the

distinguishing of good from bad. However, if you turn to her actual deeds, on the whole you will groan with the prophet and say: 'They are skilled, and they do evil. Yet they do not know how to do good.'*   *Jr 4:22*

They have at hand a superb array of laws and canons to build judgement into a holier verdict they feel will suit them best. Their mouths are a sharpened sword,* and they use   *Cf. Ps 57:4* it at their pleasure, at one time justifying the wicked, and at another taking the just man's justice away from him.* So, though this great   *Cf. Is 5:23* acuteness in their noses seems to beautify the church's countenance, being so evident, and though it seems to protect her like a well fortified tower, yet the reality is very different. It is, in fact, an extremely grave trouble for her, not only attacking her, but even taking her by assault. Are not they the ones who 'eat up' God's people 'as if they ate bread,'* and, as the word 'Damascus' suggests,   *Ps 14:4* drink innocent blood like water?*   *Cf. Ps 79:3*

5. But of course, the bride of Christ, so uniquely privileged, uses her keen perceptions to scent out the just and the unjust, the honest and the dishonest, the useful and the useless.* Like the true Emmanuel, her spouse,   *Cf. Mt 5:45* she wants to know 'how to reject evil and choose good.'* And her great sharpness is not   *Is 7:15* just in the discernment of making a judgement, but also in the decision to make a choice. When she makes a choice, she is stable in it, and what she rejects she does not hesitate to reject continually. The result is that her nose, as her spouse says, is truly 'a tower of Lebanon,'* because she aspires, with   *Sg 7:4*

all the strength of her discretion, to the whiteness of holiness, which is what 'Lebanon' means. In her opinion, this faculty is useless to her, unless she is 'whitened' by it, that is, sanctified.

Otherwise what divides irrational beasts and the living man who has the faculty of irrational reason in his instinct, except what is the natural faculty of the beast, is, in the case of man, defective because of his fallen nature; that is his unwillingness to understand for the purpose of acting rightly and the resultant defiling of the dignity of the divine image with the image and superscription of brute beasts. Hence the bride's nose is like 'a tower of Lebanon', because the tower of discriminating wisdom she has raised for herself comes from her real knowledge of holiness. In other words, she has been taught holiness not so much from example of others, or from reading books, but from her own resolute pracrice of virtue. But of course, the influence of others' example and the teaching of God's Scriptures are a great help in 'whitening' the bride, and they prepare for her in advance a great deal of the cost of that gospel temple, that must be constructed fronting Damascus.

We could quite understandably want to see 'Lebanon' as meaning the daily practice of affliction, by which the bride is made white in conformity to her spouse, since it may well be that it is from this 'Lebanon' that her spouse called her previously. 'Come from Lebanon, my bride, come from Lebanon, *Sg 4:8*   you will be crowned.'* Further, the words that come next seem clearly to favor this interpretation: 'You will be crowned,' he says, 'from the peak of Sanir and Hermon, from the dens of lions and the mountains of leopards.'* He uses these strange and various expressions to symbolize to her the different kinds of afflictions which will whiten her in very many ways until her spouse can issue his marvelous proclamation of her crowning. And this tower is all the more terrible as it faces Damascus, that is, as it faces the whole brunt of hostile power, as the height of its discretion has made it more sublime and the practise of its suffering has made it braver and more warlike.

Let these words suffice to illustrate how these words may be interpreted in praise of the church.

6. But we could also speak of any faithful soul, one to whom, all the same, 'to live is Christ',* and who has won the kiss and the embrace of the spouse. By finding pleasure in him, and recalling how she has experienced him in the past, she incessantly yearns for him with the fire of a most genuine love. She has thus gained for herself both the privilege and the name of 'bride', and so there is nothing to make us hesitate in applying to her the glory of this commendation: 'Your nose is like the tower of Lebanon.'* She has a very powerful sense of smell where her spouse is concerned, and wherever he goes she immediately tracks him down and follows him.* Not even if he goes up to heaven, not even if he goes down to hell, she cannot endure his being snatched away from her longing love.

Ibid.

Cf. Ph 1:21

Sg 7:4

Cf. Sg 3:4

But the joy of catching up and seizing, the spouse has kept for himself.

Nevertheless, so that 'bride' may be the true interpretation of her name, that is, that she may prove herself a true, intimate and sole lover of the one whom her 'soul loves,'* she hunts him down when he absents himself. To this hunting, she will give herself, wholly in all the sharpness and keenness of her sense of smell, and press on, with eager speed and tireless devotion, through the steep cliffs of the mountains, through the hollows of the valleys, through the densely wooded thickets, through the rough places in the undergrowth, scenting out his footsteps.* As long as life lasts, this is the bride's principal art, this is the refinement of what she teaches. She battles with great vigor, and in constant and tireless joy is hunting her beloved. Moreover, her frequent recourse to this holy practice, or, to put it more truly, her continual emphasis on it, has furnished her with ample supplies and wealth for the raising and constructing a dwelling for her in heaven.* It is because she is so accustomed to these practices, and so wholly experienced in them, that the bride deserves to hear her spouse saying: 'Your nose is like the tower of Lebanon.'*

7. Indeed, earlier verses in the poem expressed praise and admiration for the same qualities. The question was put to the daughters of Jerusalem: 'Who is that coming up from the wilderness, like a column of smoke, perfumed with myrrh and frankincense, with all the fragrant powders of the merchant?'* Here, of course, the words 'column of smoke'

are used because of the uprightness of her heart, raised up to heaven and knowing the 'things that are above'.* But in the later passage, on the other hand, the comparison is to a tower, because of the dauntless courage of her charity, which keeps her always consecrated on pursuing her goal, that is, her spouse in his heavenly home. It is a long time, now, since she built herself a tower at the invitation of her spouse. To construct it, she sold all that she had,* and to raise the cost of completing it, she will renounce everything.

Then, by the constant practice of humility, she built herself another tower as well, one as lofty and quite as splendid as the tower the spouse referred to earlier in the poem. 'Your neck is like the tower of David, built with ramparts.'* Here and now, however, her nose is likened to the tower of Lebanon, in other words, to the strength of her devotion, which is built up of the trees of Lebanon, scented with charity.* The scented and incorruptible height of these cedars of Lebanon can only be imagined by 'charity', which is patient, which is kindly,* which breathes to the bride's nostrils the good odor of Christ,* and never passes away, though all other woods must corrupt. The more that tower rises to the heavens, the more carefully the bride protects herself from all the vices, which she well realizes can threaten the success of her endeavors.

8. She is well aware, and never lets herself forget, what great evils Damascus has all too often brought upon the city of Jerusalem.

Cf. Col 3:2

Mt 13:44

Sg 4:4

**Cf. Gregory the Great,* Hom XL in Evan. *1.20.13;* PL 76:1166 CD.

Cf. 1 Co 13:4

2 Co 2:15

I specify hypocrisy, envy and arrogance. These are undoubtedly stains, which often attack and cast down the hearts of those who are spiritually impoverished. This is precisely why Damascus, or so they say, really means 'blood from sackcloth'; in this interpretation you can clearly understand sins of this kind, which would stain the souls of the devout, whose way of life is humble and whose penance is austere. Soft garments, the clothing of those who live in the houses of kings,* have a thicker and grosser kind of blood, the stains of greed and lust, the pomp of secular arrogance and the lust for power. The souls of the spiritual are attacked by a subtler evil, and no one could doubt that the stain here is more dangerous for being more interior. So the bride is always warning herself about 'looking toward Damascus',* never thinking she is safe on this earth until she has been admitted to the full enjoyment of the sight of her beloved.

9. But if anyone has made up his mind that it is preferable to understand the bride's 'nose' as meaning her discrimination, then I must say I feel his view is correct. It is my own view, since it was the spouse who raised in her this very lofty and well fortified tower, and it was because of it that the bride, a little while before, gloried that her spouse had 'set charity in order in her'.* The characteristic of discretion is that it defines the exact amount of every single virtue, and it restrains within fixed limits, too, the excesses and ardent impulses of charity itself.* Certainly charity is sovereign. She is rightly called the queen of

Cf. Mt 11:8

Sg 7:4

Sg 2:4

**Cf. Bernard, SC 49.5; SBOp 2:76; CF 31:25.*

the virtues, and so she is. All the same, though, charity herself does not escape the control of discretion, and she humbly submits herself to it to be regulated and kept in check. In fact, this is the very reason why charity trusts that her kingdom will last for ever, that it is ordered by the very just laws laid down by the ripe wisdom of discretion.

Hence, since discretion so ordains it, charity is always raising herself to higher things, but not thereby taking her eyes from lower things or neglecting weaker things. If she is the kind of bride who has undertaken the care of souls, then she takes their progress seriously and does not lose the wages of their salvation. On the contrary, she is always ready for action and as if she has posted herself in battle array 'facing Damascus'. She is prepared to accuse and challenge their vices, or rather, to wage war on them and take them by storm, and this is so of whatever she has seen that is not in full conformity with the rule of discretion, that is, with the 'tower of Lebanon'.

Moreover, it is to this tower, as to a sure refuge and almost like a mother's breast, that everyone has to flee when the tempter appears and his flaming spears either wound us or prepare to wound.* But if the bride is one in actuality, then she will long all the more eagerly for her spouse to be enriched. Since she has accepted that charity should be put in order within her,* then she struggles to preserve his law and ordinance in both kinds of charity, the love that she feels for her spouse, and also that which she owes her

Cf. Eph 6:16

Sg 2:4

sons and daughters. And her struggle is all for
the honor and glory of her spouse, who,
with the Father and the Holy Spirit,
lives and reigns, God,
for ever and ever.
Amen.

SERMON SEVENTY-EIGHT

The beginning of the seventy-eighth sermon.
How 'head' rightly stands for 'Christ', and
what great glory it is for the church to be
united to so excellent a head. Praise of her
'locks' follows, and they symbolize the little
ones in the church whom Christ extolls so
graciously by making it clear that they are in
some kind of way joined to him very closely.
These words of praise then commend the soul
that loves Christ, though this is the last thing
she hears when she receives a compliment.
Everything praiseworthy in her comes from
him, and her very least thought, provided that
it savors of Christ, she ascribes to him.

'YOUR HEAD IS LIKE CARMEL, and
the locks of your head are like the
purple robes of a king, joined together
by channels.'*   Sg 7:5
The spouse began his catalogue of praise,
arranged by an art known only to himself,
with her feet and her sandals,* and now he   Sg 7:1
ends triumphantly with praise of her head
and her locks. Consequently, there can be no
surer, more obvious or nobler interpretation
of the bride's 'head', than that given by the
apostle Paul. He says: 'The head of a woman
is her husband, the head of the husband is
Christ, but the head of Christ is God.'* Now,   1 Co 11:3

since the church is the body of Christ, it would be neither right nor good to consider the head of the church to be anything but Christ.

But at this point the bride may enter a secret objection, or perhaps one of her companions may object for her. For what value will there be for her in this great description made in her honor if it is only applied to her on this occasion because it belongs to each and every person in the great body of the church? And the phrase at issue is the highest point in the whole eulogy.

2. First and foremost, then, this commendation is specially fitting for that foremost bride of Christ, the church.* Up to now, the spouse has paid individual tribute to her different qualities, according to her various gifts of grace,* and at this juncture, he has bound together all the members of the one head, which is he himself. He does not want any member to vaunt itself above another, since they all share equally in the one and the same glory of their head.* But what is the reason for such a humble commendation of the head, if the head is Christ? Earlier in the poem, the bride seems to have spoken far more appreciatively, when she said: 'His head is the finest gold.'* But if we ponder, the bride is there intending to praise 'the head of Christ,' and Paul says that that is 'God'. Here, on the other hand, the spouse is concerned with the 'head of the church,' and Paul agrees that that is 'Christ'.*

3. This head he compares to 'Carmel', that is, to a mountain where there is pasture.

*Cf. Greg. Gt.,
Hom. XL in Evan.
1.6.8; PL 76:
832 AB.

Cf. Eph 4:7

Cf. 1 Co 11:3

Sg 5:11

Eph 5:23

It is a dense and fertile mountain,* where both
sheep and shepherds of sheep can find rich
pasturing, and there, too, lovers of solitude
find a suitable place for their contemplation.
In fact, scripture tells us that both Elijah and
Elisha withdrew there from the turmoil of the
world, and, under the guidance of the Holy
Spirit, handed down the ideal of a solitary
way of life to the 'sons of the prophets',* and
after, to their grandsons, which is what you
are. So the mountain of Carmel is well called
Christ, since all the degrees of the faithful
live there: shepherds of sheep with their
flocks, and men of prophetic spirit. In short,
Noah and Daniel and Job live there, repre-
senting the holiness of celibates, the discretion of pastors, and the discipline of subjects.
That mountain, which is raised aloft above
the peaks of all other mountains,* is very
rich in its abundance of fertile soil, but it also
spreads out spaciously on all sides. And for
this reason, it is also known as 'the mountain
of the Lord',* where every day the heavenly
Father builds his 'many mansions'.*

4. O LOrd, God of might and power,
O Father of glory, who will climb that holy
mountain?* Who will lie down to rest on it?
Since I have not the strength to struggle to
the heights, where the men of virtue dwell,
who will grant me to win a mansion for myself on the slopes of the mountain, at least, or
lower down, where the weak take their
stand? Let me deserve to find some kind of
place, however small, among the lowest members of this mighty head. I shall not be able to
say in excuse that my place is unworthy of

Ps 68:15

Cf. 2 K 2:3

Is 2:2

Cf. Ps 24:3
Jn 14:2

Ps 24:3

me.* It is Wisdom who holds the measuring line here, and no inequality at all will be able to make Wisdom err from the true when he measures.

If I look at my own littleness, I do indeed realize that I am nothing, but if at the greatness and beauty of the body in which I trust I belong, I can now venture to say that I am not nothing. And when I lift up my eyes to the towering crest of this body, I have at once grown enormously great, and now I cannot contain my own self. 'I shall extol you, O God my king,'* for you have taken me up into this glorious union with your body. No complaint about my unworthiness comes to me, since so renowned a head rises on high and on all sides such noble members make me a partaker in their honor. The fullness of glory it is to be made one body with this fullness, and to be part of it is to possess it all completely.

5. Happy is the bride who, at last, so that there should be nothing at all lacking to her total fullness of beauty, hears her spouse speaking of the magnificence of her head. She cannot contain her wonder at hearing him say of her: 'Your head is like Carmel.'* We are told that the meaning of 'Carmel' is 'knowledge of circumcision'. This means nothing unless it means knowing the Lord Jesus. For to know the Lord Jesus is perfect understanding, a knowledge which only the pure in heart can receive. Yes, he is the knowledge of the circumcised, the knowledge of the humble, the knowledge of the blessed. Far from that knowledge is all that is uncircumcised

and unclean, even if it unrolls all that has been written of him, from the beginning of the book right up to the end. 'Blessed are the people', he says, 'who know the joyful shout.'* Only experience can grasp knowledge of this kind, and only purity can deserve it.

Ps 89:15

So anyone who wants to have real knowledge of Jesus, and to know the mystery of Mount Carmel, must first be 'circumcised'. Not, of course, circumcised by the hand of man, which is only for one who is obviously a Jew, but with the spiritual circumcision of the heart, where the glory and the virtue come not from men but from God.* Tragic is the circumcision of the still uncircumcised! Despite all the pain of knives of stone, it has not yet cast off the reproach of Egypt.* Although there has been such agonizing tearing of the flesh, and such a great shedding of blood, the foreskin of fleshly lust is not able to be restrained in the slightest: let alone purified.

Rm 2:29

Jos 5:9

In fact, that kind of circumcision is so completely useless that anyone who submits to it, or so the apostle tells us, can receive no benefit from Christ.* 'You are severed from Christ,' he says, 'you are cut off from grace,'* because the true stone of circumcision is Christ, and true circumcision of the heart is to be justified in his grace. The more profoundly anyone cleaves to justifying grace, the more quickly he climbs Mount Carmel, and the more happily he dwells there—and Mount Carmel is Christ. And the more becomingly, too, does he adorn his head, which is the same Christ, as if with locks of hair.

Cf. Gal 5:2

Gal 5:4

6. 'The locks of your head', he says, 'are like the purple robes of a king, joined together in their tresses as they are.'* The countless number of the faithful, who cleave to Christ with sincere faith, are represented by the bride. Even if, in comparison with other members, they may seem to have less of the Spirit of God, nevertheless, when it comes to adorning their head, they are seen to have advanced more blessedly than all the others, in their own way. For, as the wisdom of Paul saw, 'those parts of the body we think least honorable, we surround with greater honor,'* and this is exactly how Christ treats his little and lowly ones. It is on their account that he cried out to his Father in the psalm: 'Your eyes have seen my imperfect parts'.*

These are the ones whose simplicity, which seems almost foolish and as if without any intelligence, the Wisdom of God has promised to enlighten. He promises to glorify it in the judgement, when he will take to himself whatever was done to the least of his little ones.* This generous interpretation takes the word 'head' as something done for the benefit of the head in service to the least parts of the body. He brings in closer contact with his own adorning the very ones whom he has drawn to his mercy, and it is not just enlightened faith that draws them, but also their holy simplicity.

So then, as is his custom, this pre-eminent giver of praise is more lavish in the way he lauds the weaker members of his body. In line with the words of the apostle, he pays them greater honor.* 'The locks of your head', he says, 'are like the purple robes of a king, joined together in their tresses as they are.'* For the very reason that they have such a lowly opinion of themselves, they abandon themselves wholly to their head and have no hope of pardon except in the passion of Christ alone. In fact, they even fear to come close to him without more support than their own selves. They never weary in seeking for patrons and go-betweens among those who stand in God's presence, subjecting them-selves to them as if to some kind of 'canals', so as to receive from them the grace of God.   *Sg 7:5*

7. This hope of theirs is not dismayed by the heavenly purple of their color. It is by these same tresses, these canals of heaven, that the dew of wonderful moisture comes down to them, making them become a kingly purple, and in this life, it is hidden from their eyes. What they are is not yet apparent to them; it is even less clear to them what they will be.* 'Beware,' says the Lord, 'that you do not despise one of these little ones.'* In the eyes of the proud, this crowd of simple people is seen as merely being very numerous, nothing more than an overgrown head of hair, yet not a hair of this head, however small, will perish.* No, I go further: there is not a hair that is not essential to the head's full beauty; without each hair, the purple robes of the eternal king will never be complete. 'Beware!'* They are not contemptible but honorable. Angels are their servants; the city of the blessed cannot be perfect if they are not there; the spouse himself, so as to be arrayed most becomingly on the day of   *Cf. 1 Jn 3:2*
Mt 18:10

Cf. Lk 21:18

Mt 18:10

Cf. Ps 81:3

festive joy,* as if with a wedding garment, has poured out his own blood to make them into a purple robe for himself.

Here on earth, they also have other channels, though of a very different character. It is through these channels that they receive lessons in faith and morals. Through these unworthy miracles, the people are consecrated to God's honor by the sacraments and rituals of the church. In a wonderful and rather terrible way, these channels of grace, which they administer, generally hold back nothing for themselves, as is usual for a channel. No, they pour wholly into the king's purple whatever they receive. Weigh up the cost of this purple for this kind of canal. Not only does the glory of the saints in heaven serve it, but here on earth, too, the

1 Co 4:1

stewards of God's mysteries* can be found serving it to their own perdition. For, just as it is part of the disorder of these channels, that they toast others with glory, but these same sacraments are for them a source of evil, as it is for the church's laymen. It is part of their infinite glory that they should never take scandal from the conduct of their ministers, but merely take salvation from their ministry.

Let this suffice for what the spouse has to say in praise of the church.

8. But if we apply these words to the soul to whom the privilege of true love has granted the favor of wedding the heavenly bridegroom, what praise could be given her, greater than all else, than that she has the same person for her head and her spouse? Far be it from

the bride's humility, consequently, to understand what is said in her honor as being thereby of less worth, because it applies it to what is common to the whole body of Christ. Perhaps, and this would be a wise measure for her spouse to adopt in her regard, he tests her humility by this praise. He certainly strengthens it, since she knows she is no more than all the rest. Clearly, even if she does tower over all the others, it is necessary to remind her that she is one of them. However far she excells all others in the purity of her love, she ought to feel beneath them in her own esteem.

At the same time, look at all the phrases in this whole eulogy. This one has been purposely kept to the very last by the spouse. Why should this be, unless to make the bride remember to refer anything in her that is praiseworthy, to her head? On this head, the heavenly Father has poured out the fullness of holy oil, and every single member of the bride, which has already been praised separately and in order, has received from the fullness* according to his capacity and at the will of the heavenly spouse. So the grace of the spouse, coming to each part according to the measure of his gift,* and has flowed down onto all that belongs to the bride. Not only is her robe, which is charity, drenched with this royal anointing, but it flows copiously onto the hem of her robe and its minutest fringes, that is, her thoughts and affections.* In fact, it would be true to say, 'all glorious is the king's daughter within', glorious in 'her golden fringes',* and that is what I think is meant in\` *Cf. Jn 1:16*

Cf. Eph 4:7

Cf. Ps 133:2

Ps 45:13

Sg 7:5

this poem by the purple locks of the bride.*

9. Indeed, according to the apostle, the woman who is a glory to her husband has been given her hair as a veil.* Now, I put it to you, surely this 'veil' is the very thing which the spouse describes as 'the purple robes of a king, joined together by channels'?* So, when the bride ponders over the things that pertain to her love for her spouse, and these thoughts are constant with her, in fact, they are all she ever thinks of, there is something else she thinks and ponders. She realizes that she is powerless to think such things of herself, as if by her own power. No, all her sufficiency is from her head, that is, from her spouse.* It is from him that there come the thickness of her locks and their beauty. And the apostle tells us that if she tends her hair carefully, it is the bridal glory,* but much more is it the glory of her spouse. It is the woman, the same apostle says, who is the glory of her husband.*

In order to please her spouse, then, the bride strives day and night to tend, arrange and dress her locks, under the guidance of her mirror. She knows that her spouse is near,* and hangs on every expression of his face. How different are the thoughts of those who immerse themselves in worldly anxiety and fleshly concerns! They meditate like a spider, never ceasing to spin spiderwebs, with which they cannot clothe themselves.* How much wiser are the bride's thoughts. She thinks upon the Most High, so as to weave for herself a web of a different kind, a purple garment, which will cover herself and her spouse. This robe has a width that can clothe both of them, and its glory is not unworthy of the king of glory.* And even though the bride knows for certain that some grace, whatever it may be and however minute, descends on her from above, from the head of the spouse, in all humility she does not refuse to place herself beneath those channels which are fit to convey to her the same kind of grace;

10. Weigh up, too, the bride's humility and wisdom, very specially commended in that phrase the spouse adds: 'Joined together by channels'.* These channels, are the holy fathers;* they are the doctors of the church; they are their institutions, writings and example. In fact, from the maidens and daughters of Jerusalem, from all sides whatsoever, the bride hastens to draw grace to herself, as she remembers having said earlier to the daughters of Jerusalem: 'Sustain me with flowers, refresh me with apples, for I am weak with love.'* So whether the spouse be announced to her by chance, by truth, through good men or bad, she uses the service of her channels, and does not worry what grace the servants and workmen possess. It is up to them to see that whatever they retain for themselves of the grace poured out in them, she has learnt to regard them as being 'ministers of Christ and stewards of God's mysteries.'*

So, she is joined to these tresses, whether they are good and the joining is in the company of the Spirit, or whether they are bad but still dispensers. Both are very necessary for her, if she is to perfect and receive to the

full that purple stain which is charity. For it
is not from the channels themselves, however
good, that she expects any grace. Grace does
not at all take its rise from them, but only
passes through them. And so she rightly refers
all the grace of the locks to the head, and
the glory of this purple to the king of glory,
who, with the Father and the Holy Spirit,
is alone 'to be praised and glorified
to all ages of ages.'*
Amen.

Dn 3:56

SERMON SEVENTY-NINE

The beginning of the seventy-ninth sermon.
How the bride's head, by another interpretation, symbolizes her mind, constantly meditating on her spouse, and the locks of her head an orderly sequence of holy thoughts. Also, it refers to the twofold change prophesied by Isaiah,* Lebanon into Chermel, and Chermel into an upland. Finally, of the two kinds of channels, which the bride uses in her work of charity, namely, the examples, teachings and prayers of the saints, and the gracious kindness of her spouse, who was made man and crucified and endured it all for her sake.

Is 29:17

'YOUR HEAD IS LIKE CARMEL, and the locks of your head like the purple robes of a king, joined together by channels as they are.'*

Sg 7:5

If you prefer to take the bride's head as her 'mind', as most scholars do, then I too am glad to meet your wishes and, if the Holy Spirit leads me, to profit you as well, by examining what this actually means. This is specially so since scripture itself in many places helps me to do this.

In fact, in this interpretation, what I hear the Lord telling us is this: that when the storm of persecution begins to rage, we must 'lift up our heads'.* In other words, we are

Cf. Lk 21:25

not in the least to let ourselves become downcast by the perplexity the sea will cause as its waves crash and swell.* We are not to wither away with fear and foreboding like other men,* but, on the contrary, lift our heads manfully on high, knowing that these are a sign of our approaching redemption.* For who is there who can hurt us? Even more, who is there who by his very persecution does not hasten on our redemption, if only we are 'zealous for what is right'?*

So the Lord ordered us to hold our heads high,* that is, to lift up our hearts, just as he himself, when 'he appeared as a high priest of the good things yet to come',* lifted up his hands to heaven, and cried out loudly to all who stood around: Lift up your hearts.* All the same, following this interpretation, we have that cry of the contrite in the psalm: 'For my iniquities have gone over my head.'* Here we have a soul sighing bitterly to God, that his sins are so great and so many that he cannot even count their number and their gravity.

2. On the other hand, at this point the spouse, wanting to praise his beloved's mind, compares her to Carmel, that is, to that lovely and lofty solitude which the noblest prophets chose for their home in days gone by. In those times, it was on Carmel that Elisha was to be found, when he was at long last drawn out of his beloved solitude by the faith of a woman, who sought for him to raise her only son.* And it was on this mountain that Elijah, father of this same Elisha, unbolted the heavens, which had long been locked, by mercifully

summoning back the clouds which in his
power he had held in check.*

Cf. 1 K 18:41

Ponder to yourselves, brothers, what great
progress these solitary men made in that
lonely place. They climbed to the very peak
of this towering mountain. How far away they
were from all the ways of the world, how
lifted up from the earth! How close they
came to heaven, these men who had the privilege of foretelling the future and raising the
dead, of ruling over kings themselves, in fact,
of making and unmaking kings! They had the
power to condemn the land to sterility at one
moment, and then at another to bless it with
growth, and then to bind and loosen the
heavens.

Moreover, these great signs of power, at
which the whole earth still marvels at this
very day, were truly signs, in that they
indicated the presence of certain enormously
great virtues in their souls. An immense light
shone so brightly within them, that these eyes
could only be described as fleeting or incon-
spicuous flashes from it. If you think of it,
within the souls of these noble men there was
a Carmel, a circumcision from all human
pleasure, from all earthly anxiety, from all
bodily desire, which is what the word 'Carmel'
signifies. For Carmel is interpreted as meaning
'knowledge of circumcision',* because those
alone know the power of this 'circumcision'
who have been privileged to experience it.

*Jerome, Liber de
nom. hebr.; PL 23:
803, 820; CC 72:
92:110.

3. Speaking of this circumcision, the
apostle sees in it a fourfold virtue. It is not to
appear outwardly, but to be hidden, in
that it has the secret of what it signifies

Cf. Rm 2:28

Rm 2:29

hidden within itself.* It is not to be in the flesh but in the spirit,* in that it is not only eager to afflict the body, but much more so to purify the heart. Then it is not the work of human hands, as if trusting in its own powers to bring itself to perfection, but it is the work

Rm 2:28

Rm 2:29

Cf. Col 1:5

of grace alone.* And finally, it is the kind of circumcision that derives its glory 'not from men but from God,'* in that it has the hope of its future glory laid up for it in the heavens, where God is.*

So these men of virtue, after zealous effort, came to have a sublime understanding of 'the knowledge of circumcision', in a way quite different from that of the Jews. Even to this day, the Jewish circumcision is in the flesh; it reveals itself only by its fleshly practices. They circumcise themselves but only to hu-man eyes. But I am not talking of that

Cf. Rm 4:1

Israel 'according to the flesh',* which is cut off from faith in Christ and from grace. No, I am speaking of those Jews who made a vow to despise the world and who trustfully set themselves to live on Carmel, glorying that they were circumcised to the world, if

Gal 6:4

not actually crucified to it.* O, if only what they boast of might be found, so that, as the Apostle says, they might truly glory 'in the

Ibid.

cross of Our Lord Jesus Christ'!* And like-wise may they glory with Elijah and Elisha to live on Mount Carmel, so as to understand, as they do, 'the knowledge of circumcision'.

4. But nowadays we see with grief that Carmel is thought of as a forest, to use the words of Isaiah. 'Lebanon will be turned into Chermel, and Chermel will be regarded as a

forest.'* (For the sake of the less learned, *Is 29:17*
I should explain that Chermel is another way
of saying Carmel, and an upland is a wood
where the trees bear no fruit.) This exchange
of nature is something very wonderful, but in
one case it is much to be desired, and in the
other it is extremely to be dreaded. Lebanon
is a very lofty mountain, densely covered
with cedars. It towers on high, proud of its
earthly glory, and on it the proud, and those
who hunger for this glory, have planted very
deeply the roots of their heart. But when the
Lord breaks the cedars of Lebanon, and shatters them like 'a calf of Lebanon',* then we *Cf. Ps 29:6*
can sometimes see Lebanon converted into
Chermel,* and the sight fills us with wonder, *Is 29:17*
and in our wonder we feel very great thankful-
ness. Anyone who has a loving knowledge of
Jesus can only be overwhelmed with amazement at these things. Such a man can hardly
contain himself for wonder and rejoicing,
when he sees the glory of this world trampled
underfoot by voluntary humility and poverty,
when he sees it slaughtered, torn in pieces
and broken, like a calf for sacrifice. There are
many wonderful examples of such a transformation, and we have heard them with our
own ears and seen them with our own eyes.
Truth so plainly revealed has no need of witnesses, but on the contrary, longs for those
who can worthily behold it and realize its
importance.

In truth, O father Isaiah, all has happened
as you promised. The desert 'has blossomed
and burst into bloom,'* and already for some *Is 35:1*
time, the lonely and pathless wilderness has

Is 35:2

Ibid.

Is 29:17

Is 35:1

Is 29:17

Am 9:3

rejoiced. 'It has exulted with joy and glad-ness.'* For, 'the glory of Lebanon has been given to it, and the beauty of Carmel.'* Obviously, the 'glory of Lebanon' is a true glory to the degree it is remote from the van-ity of its former glory and submits humbly to the lowliness of Christ, bending down be-neath his rule. And it is magnificently adorned by 'the beauty of Carmel', in other words, by the noble life the holy prophets lived, not to speak of the zeal of the apostles' poverty.

5. But what relevance has all this now? Is not Chermel regarded as 'an upland' now-adays?* I say that it is so regarded, both in the opinion of men, who think we are here for them to scorn and plunder us, and in God's verdict, because of the one thing which above all we have to fear, namely, that this solitude of ours does not blossom now as in the days gone by,* but is rather overgrown and droop-ing, an unkempt wasteland. When I hear the Lord God thundering forth the words I have already quoted, 'Chermel will be regarded as an upland,'* I am overcome with terror. I look at our solitude and see all too clearly its sterility; I gaze upon its dryness; I recog-nize the shame of these times of ours. These harsh words make me fear for myself and for you, too, my brothers, in case this fate comes upon us.

Equally terrible are these other words of God: 'Though they hide themselves on the top of Carmel, from there I shall reach out and take them.'* What can be meant by 'the top of Carmel'? Surely it is the dignity and mark of respect paid to the holy state of religion, which overtops other mountain peaks in the observance of the christian faith? But he who 'searches Jerusalem with lamps',* he searches out those who have made it their lurking place, and he 'takes them away',* when he makes the people who have gone into hiding in the past, into 'a spectacle to men and angels'.*

Cf. Zeph 1:12

Am 9:3

1 Co 4:9

But where has this lament taken me, and how much longer will it continue?

6. Certainly I have here a very fruitful theme; this verse fits in very intimately with how I feel at present, and it is highly relevant to our modern world. Yet it is the Lord's bride who must be our chief concern, lest she be deprived of her rightful honor. Even in these evil days, glory awaits her, a glory all the greater for her having been taken from the same couch on which her fellow is left, as if unworthy and rejected.* But these two act very differently when 'on their couch'.* The one spends all night seeking on her bed for 'him whom her soul loves',* while the other lies in a heavy slumber, snoring drunkenly and lost in somnolence.* And just as she passes the night tossing and turning, snorting like a drunkard and dreaming furtively, so too she also seeks and mentally searches for what her soul, sadly, loves.* Then with annoying persistence, she gets in the way of her sister, who is looking for her beloved, and she breaks in on her joy, distracting her attention and disturbing her repose. Yet, as I have said, the bride proves that she loves 'him whom her soul loves',* because this only makes her press on with greater earnestness,

Cf. Lk 17:35
Cf. Sg 3:1

Cf. Ibid.

Cf. Pr 6:9

Cf. Sg 3:1

Ibid.

while the one whom she is seeking takes her to himself with greater happiness, and when he has taken her, crowns her with greater glory.

7. Indeed, it is in reference to this present point that the spouse compares the bride's head, that is, the mind of someone who meditates only on Christ, to Carmel. He means by Carmel the blooming and exalted solitude of the fathers of old, and it is their poverty, spirit of prayer and charity that she sets herself to copy with all her strength. She submits herself devotedly to their teaching and example, as if they were channels,* and she draws more and more warmth for herself from the glowing coals which came forth from the altar of her spouse. From those who have drunk more deeply she takes what she can, some scraps of the solace provided by her beloved, but rejected by those who have had their fill, some last drop of dew caught from these same channels of grace. Although they may be very far away from her, it is with men like this that she holds continual intercourse, men whom that right of eternal light already contains, men whom the abyss of divine charity has already swallowed up. This is the same spirit that moves her, too.

Yet she rejoices that they are so very rich in what she longs for. It is a real joy to her that they have attained to the eternal enjoyment of that kiss from the mouth of her spouse, which she only deserves to snatch in passing.* In a fever, then, to be one of their company, and passionately seeking for their abundance, which she is kept from while here on earth, she does what she can, ravenous and parched. She joins herself to these 'channels', and by contemplating their blessedness, she draws off drops of the dew of their grace.

So the Lord's bride has as many channels to the things of heaven as she has mediators of grace and intermediaries of the holy covenant that binds her to her heavenly spouse; she has as many to tell her of this mutual love, to explain it to her and urge her towards it. In short, these ancient prophets are watchmen, continually keeping guard for her. She remembers that in the past they beat and wounded her,* inflicting a secret wound that nothing could heal. It was this that she revealed to the daughters of Jerusalem when she entreated and commanded them to be sure to tell her beloved, if they should find him, that she was ill.*

8. The bride has other channels too, more powerful and more sacred, and she submits herself to them with greater humility. There is more blessing in being joined to them, and what flows through them comes with greater plenty. In fact, everything that the Word Incarnate did, everything which he revealed and suffered, was a 'channel'. The only Son of God was made in the likeness of man for her, and came to her like a spouse, and he was made in the likeness of sinners for her, and crucified, and all these acts were channels for his bride, richly distilling for her the blood of that purple dye that is Christ. To these channels the bride is joined with all her energy and with the greatest, deepest devotion. She cleaves to them inseparably, she sucks them,

Sg 5:7

Sg 5:8

she keeps her tongue to them, she stirs her
heart with them, she drinks deep of their
purple, which is nothing else but the charity
of her beloved.

Her robes are of the finest purple, which
must be woven from the most delicate threads,
by which we mean holy thoughts, touching
on charity. They must be most delicately
interwoven, and they must be colored by the
purple dye of the divine sweetness, and she
keeps guard over them always. On the great
festival of her wedding day, when at last she
will enjoy to her heart's content the embraces
she so desires, she must appear in this lovely
and glorious garment, and there must be then
no 'spot or wrinkle or anything like that.'*
Moreover, on that day, when she is blissfully
joined to her spouses by those channels, she
will never have to endure a parting from him.
No, she will sing 'the mercies of the Lord of
all eternity,'* and 'the locks of her head' will
be truly 'like the purple robes of a king',
joined by channels,* joined to those channels for eternity, to the praise and glory of
her spouse, to whom, with the Father and
Holy Spirit, be glory, honor and empire
for all the ages.
Amen.

Eph 5:27

Ps 89:1

Sg 7:5

SERMON EIGHTY

The eightieth sermon here begins. Of the bride's two kinds of beauty, namely, the sanctification of her flesh and her spirit. And there are also two kinds of graciousness, that is, a careful preservation of her good reputation, and a humble acceptance of her loss of it. Also, there are three kinds of delights, namely, those they enjoy in heaven, those that belong to earth, and those which are snatched from the underworld by what we could call a devout encroachment.

'HOW BEAUTIFUL YOU ARE, how gracious, my dearest, in your delights.'*

The spouse has dwelt lovingly upon his beloved's praises, and he has now reached the point of adding a brief conclusion to what he has said. All he has praised before in detail is here summed up in brief. 'How beautiful you are,' he says, 'how gracious, my dearest, in your delights.'* Notice, first, how this master of commendation sets about it. He first pours himself out in unreserved praise of his bride, using one subtle compliment after another to make clear to the daughters of Jerusalem the marvel of such great loveliness. But then as if taking up a theme that has not yet been properly understood, he rouses and excites his

Sg 7:6

Ibid.

listeners to a completely new pitch of admiration by apparently speaking of something even greater. Granted that this particular verse is not spoken directly to the daughters of Jerusalem, but is rather addressed by the spouse to his bride herself, yet every element of this mystical marriage is discussed in the hearing of souls who seek the face of Jesus and of the holy angels. After all, anyone who is 'a friend of the spouse', certainly 'stands and listens to him', and what is heard makes him rejoice 'to hear the spouse speaking'.*

There are two circumstances here that fill even the angelic spirits with wonder. One is the bride's being taken up by such supreme majesty and so highly and repeatedly praised, and the other is the spouse's seeming to devote himself so tenderly to this task, and so completely, though the wellbeing of the universe is on his shoulders. Yet he has turned away to take up the office of loving, honoring, admiring and proclaiming this one of his handmaids. 'The heaven of heavens, and the waters that are under the heavens'* can only marvel at and glorify the greatness of God in its most gracious stooping down. Here they behold their God, the Lord of hosts, lowering himself to the point that not even they, to put it boldly, are able to fathom the depth of his humility.

2. But perhaps we should pause here, and listen more carefully to what the spouse is saying. At the very least, this may be a way to bring ourselves into the companionship of his friends. For, 'blessed are the ears that hear'* what the spouse goes on to say to the bride,

because those who pay attention are his friends, and they hear: 'How beautiful you are, how gracious, my dearest, in your delights'.* Notice first, that this beauty of the *Sg 7:6* bride has already been commended by the spouse several times. She was first praised in these terms: 'Behold, you are beautiful, my love, behold you are beautiful.'* Then we *Sg 1:14* have this: 'You are all fair, my love.'* And in *Sg 4:7* the next verses he calls her 'fair as the moon and gracious as Jerusalem.'* But now he says: *Sg 6:9* 'How beautiful you are, and how gracious.'* *Sg 7:6*

So then, when he says, 'Behold you are beautiful, my love,'* it is the bride's beauty, *Sg 1:14* which perhaps up to then lay hidden, that is being lovingly commented on by the one who 'knows what is in man'.* Moreover, both here *Jn 2:25* and also when she is called 'all beautiful'* *Sg 7:6* and compared to the moon or to Jerusalem in beauty,* the emphasis is placed on the degree *Sg 6:4* of that beauty. But in the present instance, the exclamatory 'How beautiful you are and how gracious'* seems to go beyond any *Sg 7:6* degree of admiration that can be expressed in words. The spouse can no longer endure that something so great should be confined by the narrow bounds of a comparison. No, he has left the whole affair to the reactions of his wondering hearers, and has taken care that it is received only by ecstatic admiration.

3. What makes this beauty so particularly admirable is that it aims to be 'holy in body and in spirit'.* This life on earth, which is *1 Co 7:34* wholly a trial,* she directs with all her energy *Cf. Jb 7:1* wholly to the service of her sanctification. She turns this 'body of sin' into a 'temple of

1 Co 3:16

the Holy Spirit',* and by perpetually consulting her conscience, she turns her very sins and errors into the weapons of justice, that is, into true humility. Then she can say with holy Job: 'And if it be true that I have erred, my error remains with myself.'*

Jb 19:4

How beautiful she is, therefore, carrying the treasure of her holiness intact within its fragile vessel!* She dwells like a lily among thorns, untouched by their punctures.* How beautiful she is in this, too, that her spouse enables her to overcome with love all the constraints of nature that encompass her: she makes a temple of her prison, a bridal chamber of dunghill. How clearly, by speaking like this of his bride's beauty, has the spouse apparently seen both aspects of it, and both beautifully! Obviously, there is in every soul a double aspect to holiness, for she must be 'pure of hand and innocent of heart',* that is, having the twofold holiness of flesh and spirit and striving with both to please her spouse.

Cf. 2 Co 4:7

Sg 2:2

Ps 24:4

But it is also essential for her to possess graciousness, if she is 'to please him who has enlisted her'.* The bride, too, when she praised her spouse, mentioned both these qualities: 'Behold, you are beautiful, my love, and gracious.'* Since whoever 'cleaves to God, is one spirit with him,'* the bride now receives from her spouse the identical praise she gave him, so that she may become like him in every possible way. So she too must have graciousness joined to beauty, although I think that this virtue, just like beauty, has a twofold quality. This is because it is the

2 Tm 2:4

Sg 1:15

1 Co 6:17

bride's concern to see that the purity of her reputation is preserved unscathed, for God's sake, or, if it is in any way impaired, then this impairment must be humbly and patiently accepted.

4. The bride's graciousness, then, is twofold in kind: the purity of her good reputation, as we have said, and the humble endurance of insults. Both kinds of graciousness are expressly mentioned and highly commended by the apostle when he says: 'With the weapons of justice on the right hand and on the left, in honor and dishonor, in ill repute and in good repute.'* Moreover, he speaks of both 'weapons of justice', those on the left hand as well as those on the right, so as to make it clear that war threatens on both sides, and that we need as much courage to deal with what flatters us as with what we fear.

From the praise of men there steals a subtle kind of vainglory, or it may come with greater force and clarity from the sudden heaping of praises on our head. In either case, this vainglory has all too often appeared to break the resolution of mighty men. It has been our tragic lot to see the bravest of the brave fall wounded under the edge of this sword. But then there is the bitterness of calumny, 'on the left hand',* which inflicts the wound of unwillingness to suffer, and so constantly stains and impairs our graciousness, when we guard it too feebly. I must confess, that in one way or the other, every hour sees us exposed to the wounds of our enemies; either we receive over-much flattery

2 Co 6:8

Cf. 2 Co 6:8

because of our grace, or we receive over-much embarrassment over our disgrace. In fact, as the proverb truly says, if a man is uncorrupted by success, no failure can destroy him; calumny cannot make a man lose heart unless ambition has first undermined him.*

Cf. Gregory the Great, Moralia 20.33.65; PL 76:177C.

5. For the glory of her spouse, therefore, the bride takes care to protect her graciousness in two ways. As far as the providence of God allows her, she steadily pursues what the apostle describes as 'whatever is lovely, whatever is of good repute.'* When there is obvious danger of scandal, she remembers to conceal some things from the severity of rigorous justice, as far as her sense of honor makes possible. For this is the praise which the same apostle goes on to list next,* and this is the virtue of self-control, that control is obedient to charity, while charity at the same time keeps in harmony with self-discipline; both work together, without any just complaint between them.

Cf. Ph 4:8

Ibid.

Clearly, in avoiding scandal and preserving a good reputation, the method of prudence, and the prudent method, must be to put first our duty of love for God, and second, our neighbor, for God's sake. Moreover, if scandals arise, as they necessarily will,* since it is through them that the chaff must be winnowed out and the good grain set apart, the wicked made to stumble and the good made to practise virtue, then the bride has 'a shade from the noonday sun' to protect her.* I am referring to the example of her Lord and spouse, who in similar circumstances thought nothing at all of this kind of scandal. 'Leave

Cf. Mt 18:7

Cf. Sir 34:16

them alone', he said. 'They are blind, and blind guides.'* Further, he himself became a 'stumbling block' for the proud,* and he unhesitatingly set himself in their path to make them stumble and fall. His example is a very great comfort to the bride, when she finds herself being stoned for her good works,* and hears someone being scandalized by the liberty and truth of her words. This keeps her from feeling very much afraid of scandalizing those who do indeed 'work iniquity',* and she does not take much notice of them.

Mt 15:14

Cf. 1 P 2:8

Jn 10:32

Cf. Ps. 5:5

6. But it is quite different with those who are little ones of the flock.* From contemplating their great head, whose members they are,* she learns compassion for them, and she will take the utmost care to see that she does nothing thoughtless or too imprudent that could well be a cause of scandal for them. Yet here too, though, she will see to it that all is done with discretion, so that the little one is shielded from harm without there being even the very least offense against the Lord, 'great and to be feared',* as he is.

Cf. Lk 12:32

Eph 5:23

Cf. Ps 48:1

On the other hand, there are those whom truth has not set free,* but has in fact, rather been a cause of scandal to them. If in their eyes, the bride seems to have lost her bloom, to be unbecoming and less attractive, then she can hold on to the words of Truth himself, in all his meekness. Taking it for granted, as we have explained, that the 'maidens' were daughters of Jerusalem and also little ones of his flock, she rebukes their judgement, curbs their arrogance and removes

Jn 8:32

what scandalizes them by saying: 'I am very dark, but comely, daughters of Jerusalem.'* Then she adds: 'Do not gaze at me, for I am swarthy, for the sun has scorched me,'* meaning by 'sun', the love of the truth and charity of my spouse. If my 'swarthiness' scandalizes you, in that I seem to you to have thrown away the whiteness you feel goodness demands, and if telling the truth has made me lose my attraction for you, think well. Are you not perhaps sinning against the very truth and charity of my spouse, when you reject me, your mother?

For the sake of my spouse, I can gladly bear the reproaches of those who reproach me,* as long as they do not fall on him. For it is his truth that you are attacking, it is against his truth that you are stumbling, all unknowing. But just as truth stays untouched by all your scandals, so you cannot violate my graciousness whatever your reproaches, whatever your foul suspicions or whispered calumnies. And even if my good reputation, which on this earth can never remain unchanged, were to suffer some loss, 'it seems to me a very small thing to be judged by you or by man's day.'* My graciousness would still be mine, whole and unblemished, and I would feel not the slightest loss to it, for all the mangling of men. In fact, I would take these attacks as positively contributing to make my graciousness more graceful!

So it is a glad and fitting thing that this fairest of women should hear her beloved praise and congratulate her: 'How beautiful you are and how gracious.'* The grace of her

Sg 1:4

Sg 1:5

Cf. Rm 15:3

1 Co 4:3

Sg 7:6

beauty is so great that it keeps her holy in soul and body. In the same way, it watches with every care over the health of her good name. When it is attacked, because it is hers, it helps her to bear the wounds humbly and courageously, and in both cases alike, it makes her grow in graciousness all the more.

7. Then come the words: 'My dearest, in your delights.'* Dear in beauty, dearer in graciousness, 'dearest in delights'.* She is dear to her spouse when she sets about her own salvation, a holy woman anxious to become yet more holy. She is dearer when she also takes on the task of helping her brother, not only trying to be no obstacle to anybody but actively building them up as christians. But she is dearest when she is only concerned with her beloved, with his embraces and kisses, his addresses, his anointings, his fragrance. All these and other secrets that are the lovely bliss of marriage, she knows by foretaste, when they are present, savoring them in her spirit with a most intimate sweetness! And when they are not present, she searches for them, earnest and tearful.

Yes, these are the delights that the bride knows so fully when the left hand of her spouse is under her head, and his right hand embraces her.* But they are also delights when she languishes without him on her bed,* when she searches through the streets and squares of Jerusalem for her vanished spouse,* leaving no stone unturned in heaven or earth or even under the earth as long as somewhere, anywhere, she may find the one she seeks.* Certainly, she never rests from

Jn 1:18

pondering and brooding over the glory of her beloved, who ascended into heaven and reclines in his royal ease, namely, in the Father's bosom.* She ponders on the eternal years which are his in heaven, hoping that from the full glory where her spouse dwells, something heavenly may glide into her soul, as she contemplates these things of heaven.

But if she finds herself driven away from there, disappointed in her divine longings, she makes straight for the delights she reads of in scripture: 'My delights are to be with the sons of men.'* And she reads also: 'And darkness was my light in my delights.'* O what words of bliss! A love so incredible deserves to melt the hardest heart, however adamant its flint. 'My delights', says the king of glory, the only Son of the Father, 'My delights', mark you, 'are to be with the sons of men.'* 'And darkness was my light in my delights.'* Wake up, my soul, why let sleep still weigh you down? 'Sons of men, why still so heavy of heart',* why still so unaware of the delights of a charity so great? Why still let yourselves be led away from these true and real delights by delights that are rotten and corrupt? For the race of men has true and real delights, since 'the Word was made flesh and came to live among us.'* Delights are true and real since our creator stooped to become our head,* by taking on our flesh. By suffering our death, he has even stooped to become our reward.

8. Here are two kinds of delight, and every holy soul is ceaselessly concerned with them and strives to practise them. The more frequently and sweetly she calls to mind the

richness of this twofold pleasure, the more subtly sensitive to delight she becomes. To enjoy it more easily and joyously, she tries to banish and drive far away from her all the delights of this world, like so many flies that destroy the sweetness of a perfume. She has no desire at all to hear that dread reproach: 'How long will you shake off delight, O faithless daughter?'* And equally terrible to hear would be: 'Go out, and follow in the tracks of the flock, and pasture your kids beside the shepherds' tents.'* So when the bride is thus driven away from the delights of heaven, she is forced to seek ever after her spouse in the delights he recalls as having been his among the sons of men, when he lived among them* and endured the darkness* of the cross and of death for them.

Jr 31:22

Sg 1:7

Jn 1:14
Cf. Mt 27:45

9. But if even here she cannot come upon the spouse, then the bride does not hesitate even to go down to the underworld, in case she is fortunate enough to find him there. For his power unfolds itself to the bride in her constant meditation; the dark places of the underworld were wonderfully lit up by the brightness of his coming and he led out of the darkness the flock he had captured 'with a strong arm and an outstretched hand',* taking the powers of hell triumphantly and gloriously into captivity. From all this, she derives some deep and solemn joy. But there is also the fact that she herself has been rescued from the underworld by the tender love of her spouse. The first grace he gave her was to visit her and set her free, and her meditation on this is ever new and

Ps 136:12

intimate and repeated.

Whenever she is allowed to rejoice with the Lord her God over these things, she recalls with eager heart where she came from and where he has now brought her, and it seems to her that in the middle of the underworld, Jesus is with her. These may be lowly delights, inferior in degree, and yet the bride does not despise them. Anything that tastes of Jesus, she finds all delight and wholly sweet. To Jesus Christ, then, author of this beauty, this graciousness and these delights, be honor,
glory and power, together
with God the Father and
the Holy Spirit, for
ever and ever.
Amen.

SERMON EIGHTY-ONE

The beginning of the eighty-first sermon. Of the bride's stature, and the threefold significance of stature; and the reason why her stature, that is, her steadfastness, is compared to this particular kind of tree. Next, of the bride's breasts, that is, her twofold practice of charity, the milk from which is sweet to encourage and to comfort. Anyone who has not these breasts has no right at all to claim the title of bride.

'YOUR STATURE IS LIKE the palm tree, and your breasts are like clusters of grapes.'*   Sg 7:7

At the moment, three ways occur to me of understanding the bride's 'stature', and its likeness to a palm tree. It is for you to decide which of them is the most effective, though of course, you may have something even better to propose. Well then, I suggest that 'stature of the bride' is either her undeviating steadfastness, or else her persevering confidence, or else the unconquerable steadiness of her humility.

Steadfast righteousness is, in fact, compared to the palm tree in another place, by the Holy Spirit, when he says: 'The just man will flourish like the palm tree.'*   Ps 92:12
Moreover, the just, whose 'souls are in God's hands',*   Ws 3:1
and who are clad in robes of white,* were seen   Rv 7:9

Ibid.

Ibid.

Mt 21:8

Sg 7:6

Ws 5:17

in a vision by St John. He saw them standing before the Lamb,* and they are described as as having held palms in their hands, clear token of their triumphant steadfastness.* So, when the Son of David held his triumph, the Hebrew children are said to have run to greet him with palm branches.* They were using these sacred symbols to proclaim the victory of Christ's righteousness and outstanding steadfastness.

In the athletic contests of the past, those who strove according to the rules received a crown made from the branches of this tree, and ever since it has become the custom to call victory in any kind of contest the 'palm'. So it comes very fittingly among the bride's titles of honor, that after mention has been made of her beauty, graciousness and 'delights',* that there should be explicit praise of her steadfastness and truth. Her invincible courage is given prominence, to show that she is worthy of her crown, like one who has duly struggled very often for the cause of right. For the bride does not expect that her righteousness will be wholly crowned only on the day when she receives 'the crown of glory from the hand of her God'* and spouse. No, she knows with unshakeable faith that on this earth too, she will have from her spouse a crown for every single contest she has waged.

2. But it is highly appropriate that she is not said to be holding palm branches in her hands or twined about her head. Rather, her stature is compared to the whole tree. The implication is that she has roots like the palm, flowers and bears fruit and finally perseveres a very long time, like the palm. She is rooted

like a palm, for she has set her deep and immovable desire and purpose on an eternal crown. She grows like a palm, since she usually begins harshly, because of her austere way of life, and then, at full height, becomes gentler, because of her goodness and sweetness. She bears flowers like a palm, when she seems to bear already the first blossoms of her coming fertility, being fragrant with hope. Then she bears fruit like a palm, for she knows, here below, the most blessed fruit of eternal happiness. And finally, she lives for many years, like the palm, in that the strength of her righteousness is invincible, and her crown can never fade.

Likewise, we must realize that at certain times the bride is not without her combats, even though her spouse hides her very lovingly in the secret of his face from the turmoil of men and their lying tongues.* He shelters her, as Isaiah says, as a man tries to shelter himself from the gale, hiding as best he can from the blast.* She knows well that her spouse promises peace, but it is his peace, not the world's, that he gives.* In fact, the world takes up a position of hostility to her, and always sets itself in opposition to wreak its spite. But her spouse has arranged this for her good, to make her stature like that of the palm tree;* if she always has something to fight against, she will always be able to overcome. So, however many battles with her antagonists come to her from the world, all of them mean just so many palm trophies to be received from the generosity of her spouse. And even if the world were to keep silent,

Cf. Ps 31:20

Cf. Is 32:2

Jn 14:27

Sg 7:7

there is no silence for her from the enemy within or from 'her who sleeps within her bosom'.* The country of the soul is never at rest from interior warfare, so that there is no end to the number of her palms, just as there is none to the number of her combats.

3. So there is a true likeness between her stature and the palm, a tree that stands so firm and so unshaken. Further, these constant trials make her continually grow like a palm. I repeat, she is truly like a palm tree, because repeated victory makes her not merely a victor or victorious but makes her into the victory itself: she herself becomes a crown of glory. For it is not the flattering voice of false praise but the true admiration of the Holy Spirit that proclaims: 'You will be a crown of glory in the hand of the Lord, and a royal diadem in the hand of your God.'* It seems to me that it is in this sense, because it is meant in the same spirit, that the bride's stature, as we said, is compared to the palm tree. She has been the victor in so many battles that she has earned the glory of this title here on earth, and deserves to be called 'palm', or crown.

But in the exertions that are part of all these combats, nothing strikes me as more difficult, calling for more courage, and finally, more successful than what we find described in scripture. The quotation I mean says: 'I thought of my God, and was delighted; I was harassed, and my spirit failed me.'* The words 'and my spirit failed me', are a clear expression of real difficulty and the weariness of the struggle. Should this surprise us? Her contest is with an angel, and until the angel is overthrown, the palm cannot be hers.* In fact, we could say that the real antagonist in this struggle is the Lord God of hosts, and until he consents to be worsted, and only then, will the longed for end of the combat dawn.* *Cf. Gn 32:24*

Cf. Gn 32:31

But indisputably, the more his bride is forced to grapple with this situation, the more frequently she triumphs. Her struggles lead her in ever more ardent pursuit of the delights that flee from her, to the point that she at last deserves not merely to speak with her spouse, but to receive his embrace and his kiss. It follows from the remarkable steadfastness of her combat, and her repeated victory in the battle, that her stature is indeed comparable to the palm tree. As we have observed, she never ceases making steadily for her goal, or rather, she never ceases until she reaches it. In this most blessed kind of combat, she is careful to train and exercise whomever she can, provided, of course, that she sees in them a spirit that can rise to this challenge. She watches well to make sure that they will act worthily, and not be too cowardly to embark upon this battlefield.

4. This is why, when the spouse has said: 'Your stature is like a palm tree,' he expressly adds: 'and your breasts are like clusters of grapes.'* If her love is genuine, she ought to be ready to bare the breasts of her love and offer them to those who, as we have described, are able to receive them in so far as they too are lovers. The charity of God is never idle, it is never heedless, especially of its blessed and *Sg 7:7*

glorious offspring. Being great itself, it sets great things in motion, longing to pour itself into the hearts of those with whom it is tenderly united. Love is truly a sharing in the Holy Spirit, and the more a man has of it, the more it urges him to share it with others.*

Cf. 2 Co 13:13

So the two breasts of the bride are the movements of a twofold charity, and it is because of them that the bride is raised so incontrovertibly above all those who love. Indeed, the very first line of this poem indicates how passionately she is inflamed with love of God, for she says there: 'Oh, that he would kiss me with the kiss of his mouth!'* Everything that she has to say in the same vein makes it quite clear that 'out of the heart's abundance, the mouth speaks.'* Then there are the expressions of infinite sweetness that she uses when she is in company with the daughters of Jerusalem, clear evidence of her praiseworthy love for her neighbor. She generously reveals to them how love has wounded her, not concealing that her soul has melted away under the force of her beloved's words.* She sweeps them into partnership with her endeavors, doing her very best to ensure that they too will be quick to follow in her footsteps.

Sg 1:1

Mt 12:34

Sg 5:6

What do you make of it? Does it not seem to you that she offers the daughters the breasts of a twofold love? Just as she herself strives to love both her spouse and them, so she would have them love, also. The milk in these breasts can only be the sweetness of this twofold love, and what they draw from these breasts can only be the sweetness flowing from it. Although the spouse declares that they abound, not with milk, but with wine, and this is why he has compared her to clusters of grapes.* *Sg 7:7*

5. In fact, the marriage song opens with these words of the maidens to the bride: 'Your breasts are better than wine.'* It seems *Sg 1:1* to me that those who are not yet able to take the 'better drink' are delighted when it is mixed in with the nourishing milk from their mother's breasts, and they are rejoicing that she is training them in accordance with their capacity. But the time has now come when their daily intercourse with her has enabled them to receive in fuller measure. As Solomon says, 'Iron sharpens iron, and one man sharpens another,'* and the maidens have now *Pr 27:17* come to know Christ, not according to the flesh but, to quote the apostle, 'according to the Spirit'.* Not only in their hearts but in *Cf. 2 Co 5:16* their souls, that is, not only in their tender affections and loving memories, but with all their soul's strength, they have come to love Christ. Now they are able to think it blessed to suffer for Christ,* and to endure the bitter- *Cf. Ac 5:41* ness of any trial for the sake of justice, of truth, of obedience, of the good of their brothers.

Very possibly it is this that the spouse wanted to emphasize when he followed his comparison of the bride's stature to a palm tree by comparing her breasts to clusters of grapes. For having reached that pitch of patience and steadfastness where she could begin to glory in her sufferings* and, with the *Cf. Rm 5:3*

2 Co 2:14

apostles, render thanks for them to God, who always causes her to triumph in Christ Jesus,* and thereby to be called the palm of victory itself (for she had already earned the prize of

Cf. Is 62:3

being the crown of glory in God's hand*); from that moment she abounds in consolations for all those who seek Jesus. The breasts of the same grace Paul rejoices to have received when he said to the Corinthians that he was able to console those who were suffering every

2 Co 1:4

kind of anguish.* The source and giver of this gift of consoling others he revealed a little before, when he blessed God who had also consoled him in all his trials so that he might

Ibid.

be able to console others who are suffering.* So, to quote the spouse, Paul's stature is comparable to the palm tree, and in consequence he has breasts that could be likened to clusters of grapes.

6. But no mother, however fruitful, can have her breasts compared to that new and perfect wine that Jesus promised he would keep for his disciples to drink with him in 'my

Mt 26:29

Father's kingdom'.* That wine flows from the breasts of the spouse, not from the breasts of his bride. That is a joy for the future, to relish to the blissful limit those vessels of

Ps 144:13

wine, 'overflowing with every possible good.'* Here and now, our task is to cling to the breasts of the bride and receive, after a while, a taste of that wine, not of course in its purity, but with the grape skins still in it. The skins and stones of the grape are the cloak of words, the wrappings of imagery, riddling comparisons and obscure maxims. Obviously, to use clusters of this kind is both intriguing and helpful here on earth, since they are both the food and drink which prepare us for the purity of the heavenly marriage feast.

However, the cluster intended there may be a cluster of henna blossom, for we have the bride saying: 'My beloved is to me a cluster of henna blossom.'*   *Sg 1:13*

7. In the promised land, the clusters were extraordinarily sweet and large, and the scouts who went into that glorious country brought back to their own land a report of their richness.*   *Cf. Nb 13:26*   O blind race of men! Moses sent you ahead to explore the fertility and beauty of that country, and you bring nothing back in reply except hunger and death.*   *Cf. Nb 13:32*   You have taken no notice of the vineyard of the Lord of Hosts, that well-designed plantation is the angelic host. You are a race of unbelievers, unable as yet to realize that the man, of Judah is his sweet planting, the cluster of henna blossoms the beloved of the daughters of Zion. But though you neither desire it nor know it, you bring back a report of it to the race that will come after you. To this very day, the Vine is in your midst, but still, blind unhappy race, you do not see him. You only feel the weight of him, but never profit from him, never savor him. He is the lightest of all burdens*, but you have made him into one   *Mt 11:30*   that is very heavy. You have turned him into a weight that animals should bear, not men. You feel you are forced to bear him, and so his weight presses on your backs and brings you his refreshing drink.

8. Therefore, being rejected yourself, you have been the cause of bringing in glory new

delights for the new bride. So the woman made for joy can delight as if all riches and delights were hers, and in her delight can say: 'My beloved is to me a cluster of henna blossom.'* From this cluster she is filled to capacity, from this cluster she prepares her banquet, from this cluster she makes her feast. She drinks from it, refreshes her inmost being on it, delights her palate with it. From it she fills her breasts, to make them become like 'clusters'. For there is nothing the bride seeks to say or to teach except only Jesus. Only Jesus, whether born of the Father or brought forth by his mother, whether living among men or suffering on account of men or reigning already with his Father, 'from now and for ever more.'*

This is how any faithful soul can prove that she is a true bride: if she is, then her beloved will be to her as a cluster of henna blossom between her breasts, dwelling within her breasts and inebriating his own.*

9. But it may be that she has not Jesus continually in her heart and often on her lips, that she cannot say, when she will: 'Your name and your memory is the desire of my soul',* and 'my tongue will recall your justice, your praise all the day long.'* It would be wrong indeed for a soul like that to try to claim for herself the title or the glory of being 'bride'. A bride is one who loves, but one who loves deeply, who burns with love, who faints, who fails, who clings, who chooses to know nothing except Jesus alone.*

The spouse explains that the sign of his coming can be read in the figtree, meaning, from the sign of its young branches and new leaves.* But these young tender branches really mean the tenderness of a heart thinking of Jesus, and the new leaves are consoling and loving talk about Jesus. These leaves spread wide, and they are a sign that very sweet fruit is to follow; they never fall away, they never wither. And so, with their shade, they are a fine screen for the bareness of our transgressions. This is specially so when the fig is of the kind that wants to show not only leaves but also fruit to Jesus when he comes to find fruit on it.*

Mt 24:32

Mt 21:19

So the bride's breasts, overflowing with rich teaching about Jesus, and his consolation, can well be compared by the spouse to clusters of grapes. Their fertility comes from him who praises them, the Son of God, who,
    with the Father and the Holy Spirit,
      lives and reigns, God,
        for ever and ever.
          Amen.

SERMON EIGHTY-TWO

The beginning of the eighty-second sermon.
Why steadfastness has been called 'stature', and
how the bride's patience or humility may also
be described as 'stature'. Then, of the fourfold
dimensions of Christ's charity, and how the
bride's charity, in its own degree, corresponds
equally with four dimensions. Also, what the
fruits are, which the spouse declares he has
seized, for the bride to use. How these same
words are especially applicable to the martyrs,
but after them, to the whole church.

'YOUR STATURE IS LIKE the palm
tree, and your breasts are like clusters
of grapes.'*

Sg 7:7

We could have moved on to the next verse,
and spared both your fatigue and my labors,
if I had not myself fallen into the snare of my
own words. I cannot forget that the day
before yesterday I set squarely before you the
meaning we must here assign to 'stature', and
that we were concerned in that sermon with
one of these meanings, two others still remain-
ing undiscussed.

We need no longer weary ourselves in
explaining why we spoke there of the virtue
of steadfastness, which we said was what
'stature' signified and which was compared
by the spouse to the stature of the palm tree,

for the reasons given above. Moreover, you yourselves are not lacking in insight, being men who, by the grace of God, have very frequently read and listened to scripture, and been endowed thereby with insight, and this for some years. When scripture says, 'Matathias and his sons took up a steadfast posture',* the word 'posture' is intended to convey their steadfastness. Paul, too, when he says, 'Stand fast therefore, and do not submit again to a yoke of slavery,'* and again, 'Be vigilant, stand fast in the faith,'* wants to emphasize steadfastness in freedom and in the faith. He says many other things along these lines, as you can observe for yourselves. And when the Lord spoke through Isaiah, urging his disciples to steadfastness by the example of his passion, his words were: 'Let us stand fast together.'* I could give many instances, but let these few suffice, so that we can move on quickly to other things.

2. Well now, let us see whether patience or humility could not also be described as the bride's 'stature', and be equally compared to the palm tree. In point of fact, right through the scriptures stature is repeatedly spoken of as meaning the perseverance of patience. It is in this sense that the psalmist puts perseverance before us, either in praise or recommendation, when those who 'stand in the house of the Lord, in the courts of the house of our God,'* are called upon to bless or praise the Lord. At the very beginning of the psalms, he defines the blessed man as one who 'does not stand in the way of the sinful',* meaning, one who does not linger there for

1 M 2:16

Gal 5:1
1 Co 16:13

Is 50:8

Ps 134:1

Ps 1:1

long. Scripture teems with similar quotations, and there is no need to go through them all again, since you know them.

In the same fashion, scripture refers to the humility of the just man who 'stood in the breach before him, to turn away his wrath from destroying' Israel.* And there is also a reference to humility in the words: 'John stood.'* Likewise: 'The friend of the bridegroom stands and listens to him, and rejoices to hear the bridegroom's voice.'* Then the book of Revelations has this to say about even the humility of the spouse: 'See, I stand at the door and knock.'* This is very similar to what the bride says about her beloved: 'See, there he stands, behind our wall.'* In both instances, it is his infinite humility that is being commended, for he waits modestly at the door of his servants or behind his handmaid's wall, as if he were one of the household slaves, or a member of the tribe of beggars. He stands there knocking and waiting, until a reply comes or the door opens. When scripture speaks of the holy living creatures seen by Ezekiel, it says that 'when they stood still, they drooped their wings,'* which should be taken as a clear reference to their humility.

3. What we should rather examine is why the bride's patience or humility is compared to the palm tree. There is a proverbial saying that this type of tree lives longer than others, as Isaiah remarks: 'Like the days of a tree, shall the days of my people be.'* The reference here is believed to be to the palm tree, if one takes the words literally, as this tree seems to exhibit a sort of patience or

Ps 106:23

Jn 1:35

Jn 3:29

Rv 3:20

Sg 2:9

Ezk 1:24

Is 65:22

eternity, so long does its old age continue.
This is what holy Job means when he says:
'I shall multiply my days like the palm.'* *Jb 29:18*
There is, all the same, one point in which this
same tree is unlike all others, and that is that
its lower regions are lowlier than theirs. It
follows the law of humility: 'The greater you
are, the more you must humble yourself in
everything.'* So, then, it is either one or both *Sir 3:20*
of these aspects of this virtue that the beloved
praises, using the image of this tree. His soul
loves one who tries so faithfully to be loving,
just as she herself recalls that she is at every
moment the beloved of her beloved. She
remembers what scripture says of him, that
'having loved his own who were in the world,
he loved them to the end.'* *Jn 13:1*

Think, now, whether it may not perhaps be
Christ himself, who is this palm. It is he who
has deigned to compare the patience of the
bride's love as being as great as the patience
of his charity. No stylist or master of rhe-
toric could find a greater or more meaningful
simile in heaven or on earth to which to
compare the love of his beloved, whether in
its strength or in its patience or in its humility.
If we are treating of the strength and con-
stancy of Christ's love, we find scripture saying of it: 'Love is as strong as death.'* If it is *Sg 8:6*
his love's patience, then there is the quotation
recently cited, that Jesus loved 'to the end'.* *Jn 13:1*
(And not merely to the end of this mortal
life, but to the end of immortal and blessed
life.) If we turn to his humility, it was in this
connection the apostle spoke of Jesus 'empty-
ing himself',* and it was for that reason that *Ph 2:7*

he 'became obedient to the Father, even to death, the death in fact of the cross.'*

Ph 2:8

4.   Surely this is a reference to the mystery of Christ's love, which is completely beyond our understanding? Paul knelt down to beseech 'the Father of our Lord Jesus Christ'* that the Ephesians should be able to 'understand what is the length and breadth and heighth and depth' of this love.* The length, as we have said, may be taken as its long-suffering patience, the long continuance in love that endures to the end. The breadth is the extent of that love, which enabled so great a God to undergo gladly for our sakes death and the pains of death. The depth could well be taken as referring to that vast abyss of humility which made him choose to be numbered with the guilty* and to die on the cross of the guilty, all for the sake of the guilty. As for the height, what seems to me relevant here is what the spouse said immediately after the words under discussion: 'I said: I will climb the palm tree and lay hold of its fruits.'* The 'fruits' of this palm are high indeed, eternal glory and the indescribable joy of the most blessed vision of God, the blissful company of the citizens of heaven and everything good in the 'land of the living',* which 'eye has not seen nor ear heard nor has it entered the heart of man to conceive'.*

Eph 3:14

Eph 3:18

Is 53:12

Sg 7:9

Cf. Ps 27:13

1 Co 2:9

This palm tree, then, is charity, most deeply rooted, extended very widely, living on to endless ages, bearing fruit to the glory of the kingdom of heaven, and, as we have pointed out, it is the charity of Christ Jesus, who means to plant his beloved's love after the likeness of his own. In fact, he made her sit down to a great feast, which made it incumbent on her to lay before him a similar banquet.*

Lk 9:14

5. But how can this be in her power? What adequate requital could there be to such tremendous love? What comparison would not seem absurd? However great the love of any rational spirit, how can he repay the Lord?* Even take this one point alone: that Jesus redeemed his life from the grave* by giving up instead his own life, making himself the redemption price for her soul.* Is it any wonder that the noble body of apostles and the great army of martyrs are one and all concerned to pay so huge a debt? So great is their concern that when the cup of Jesus comes down from heaven into their hands,* their reaction is one of immense joy.* They do not feel like those who are dealing on equal terms, but rather as those who are privileged to return like for like, as far as they are able. Whatever the benefits granted them, this in itself was by far the greatest and most glorious, that they were thought worthy to endure insults, torture and at last, death itself, for the name of Jesus.* Listen to the apostle: 'For God has granted you not only to believe in him, but even to suffer for his sake.'*

Cf. Ps 116:12
Cf. Ps 103:4

Cf. Ps 49:8

Mt 20:22
Cf. Ac 5:41

Ibid.

Ph 1:29

6. So the martyrs, too, looking at this great gift of God, go on to ask how they can repay the Lord* for a cup so full of salvation and of glory. By draining it, they have been healed of all their weakness and finally made comparable in glory to Jesus, that lofty palm.

Ps 116:11

Even further, what measure or amount of repayment could there be when everything that these chosen ones are given and which they repay, is recognized as wholly unearned, so much so that what is given in return for grace, is itself a grace. All we possess, God has freely given in advance, and then he goes on to give still more, he gives us glory by 'crowning us with mercy and compassion'.* All the same, while we are all in debt, whatever the amount that has been given or received, no section of the church has been likened to Christ the palm tree in the way that the martyrs have been likened. It is the martyrs, carrying palms of victory from the field of battle, who are privileged to appear before in the sight of God's glory, and there, before the throne of God and the Lamb, who is the true Victor in them, cast down their crowns.*

So it is to the bride, returning from the combat to her fatherland, bride of the Lamb, offering to her heavenly spouse the blood-red marks of her passion, that the Lamb signals out for the praise we heard quoted from this song the previous day: 'The locks of your head are like the purple robes of a king, joined together in their tresses as they are'.* This applies to what we are now discussing also: 'Your stature is like the palm tree.'* The interior meaning of this is that he is telling her that he wants to acknowledge her before his father, since she has acknowledged him before men.* But you can see without difficulty how shaken down and even running over is the measure of this exchange of compliment,*

Cf. Ps 103:4

Cf. Rv 4:10

Sg 7:5

Sg 7:7

Cf. Mt 10:32

Cf. Lk 6:38

since her acknowledgement was passing and only before men, while his is eternal and before God.

7. So, as I have said, it is this martyred section of the church, although its comprehension is like that of all the saints,* that comprehends more profoundly than the others one thing: 'what is the width and length and heighth and depth' of the love of Christ.* For it comprehends by understanding, and it comprehends by loving: it comprehends in heart and in action. So it strove not indeed to make its stature equal to his in these four dimensions, but simply to become like it, in breadth by the generosity of its suffering, in length by perseverance in unending struggle, in height by the boast of its future hope in the midst of battle and finally in depth by the lowliness of its self-esteem when it leaves the field victorious.

Certainly, for all the martyrs, whether they were preparing themselves for their trial or were actually experiencing its agonies or were now at last triumphing over them, the only reply that came from their own weakness was that of death. Every single martyr exclaimed with overpowering force: 'All men are untrustworthy'.* The true meaning of their words was that it is not within the power of human wisdom to acknowledge Christ before the judgement seat of kings, and the terrible sight of pains and torture; it is not within the power of human strength to reply as a christian should, when it comes to questioning on the rack. No, they say, it must be God's gift, if in that hour I am not untrustworthy but a true and incontestible witness. It is God who puts wisdom into the mouth, which no human wisdom or eloquence can withstand, it is God who gives a strength and wisdom which no human or even angelic power can resist.

The humility of the martyrs, then, presumes on nothing human. They fix the anchor of their hope firmly in the abyss of the divine goodness, and this humility is the 'depth' of their charity, just as we might call it the unshakeable basis of their stature and the immovable root of their palm tree. So it is specially apt to compare the martyrs to this Christ-palm tree, since they have so fully and truly expressed their likeness to Christ's charity by bearing the burden of their cross. This is why the martyrs eat in glory the fruits of their palm, and enjoy the labors of their hands, free now from the sweat of their brow.* For eternity they glorify Christ, in whom they became strong, or rather, who for them and in them, ascended the palm tree, to pluck its fruit and set it before them.*

8. Moreover, there is great praise, too, in this sentence, for the bride of Christ, who today lives in peace of one kind or another. But in fact, though she may have escaped the swords of the persecutor, she has not escaped tribulation, she has not escaped difficulties, she has not escaped calumny and reproach, perils from false brethren, warfare abroad or anxieties at home.* Look well: in this peace of hers, the bitterness is very bitter.* It is understandable that she blesses the days of the martyrs; the persecutor who sought their

mortal life also put to death the concupiscence in them. First the sword of their enemy
killed them with their concupiscence, and
then it sent them up to heaven to be victorious for ever. But nowadays, though the
earth may be at rest from battle, it is not at
rest from viciousness, and, as wise men know,
because we are granted life, we take pleasure
in sin. Literally, the sword long ago returned
to its scabbard, at the Lord's command,* but,   *Cf. Jn 18:11*
to our shame, it was to a sword far more
cruel and much more terrible that the Lord
said: 'Come forth: go to the right hand and
the left, wherever your edge is directed.'*   *Ezk 21:16*

So it comes about that today this sword
rages freely throughout the whole church,
sparing no rank, office or order. And still,
among such a huge throng of the called, it is
an establisehd fact that there are not a few
who are chosen,* who have not bent their   *Cf. Is 14:1*
knee to Baal.* Or, if they have bent it, they   *1 K 19:18*
have manfully straightened up and retracted
their submission, paying to their God the
reverence they owe to his presence. But
for these chosen few, the faithless crowd that
surrounds them, that presses close about
them, that hems them cruelly in, is like a torture press. It is like the flails of the threshing
floor, like a mass of persecutors, like a sword
sharpened for martyrdom. Surely these too
have a right to say today: 'How many trials
you have shown me, how many evils, yet you
have raised me up only to cast me down.*   *Ps 71:20*
In giving me peace, you have taken peace
away from me. Nevertheless, this is how it
must of necessity be, and the virgin daughter

of Zion could come to her full measure of stature in no other way. Only in this way can she become like the palm tree of Christ, comparable either to the glory of the afore-mentioned martyrs or the patience and love of her spouse.

9. We read that, during his passion, our Lord was clothed by his persecutors in two different garments, one white* and one pur-ple.* Herod put the white one round him, and Pilate the purple. Herod, true enough, did not torture him, but he pursued him with mockery and contempt. Pilate put him to the test with scourgings, blows and buffetings, and then sent him on to be crucified. Both occasions were noble instances of martyrdom, one showing the martyr's triumph, the other the confessors' martyrdom. A purple garment is the lot of the physical martyrs, while for the confessors there is white, but in both, the work is accomplished by Jesus, who for them both 'went up into the palm tree'.* He plucked its fruit,* too, and at his pleasure hands it out to both, he who is the spouse
of the church, Jesus Christ our Lord,
who with God the Father and
the Holy Spirit, lives and
reigns God for ever
and ever.
Amen.

Cf. Lk 23:11

Cf. Jn 19:2

Sg 7:8

Ibid.

CISTERCIAN PUBLICATIONS INC.

TITLES LISTING

THE CISTERCIAN FATHERS SERIES

THE WORKS OF BERNARD OF CLAIRVAUX

Treatises I: Apologia to Abbot William, On Precept and Dispensation . . . . CF 1

On the Song of Songs I–IV . . CF 4, 7, 31, 40

The Life and Death of Saint Malachy the Irishman . . . . CF 10

Treatises II: The Steps of Humility, On Loving God . . . . CF 13

Magnificat: Homilies in Praise of the Blessed Virgin Mary [with Amadeus of Lausanne] . . . . CF 18

Treatises III: On Grace and Free Choice, In Praise of the New Knighthood CF 19

Sermons on Conversion: A Sermon to Clerics, Lenten Sermons on Psalm 91 . . . . CF 25

Five Books on Consideration: Advice to A Pope . . . . CF 37

THE WORKS OF WILLIAM OF SAINT THIERRY

On Contemplating God, Prayer, and Meditations . . . . CF 3

Exposition on the Song of Songs . . . CF 6

The Enigma of Faith . . . . CF 9

The Golden Epistle . . . . CF 12

The Mirror of Faith . . . . CF 15

Exposition on the Epistle to the Romans . . . . CF 27

The Nature and Dignity of Love . . CF 30

THE WORKS OF AELRED OF RIEVAULX

Treatises I: On Jesus at the Age of Twelve, Rule for a Recluse, The Pastoral Prayer . . . . CF 2

Spiritual Friendship . . . . CF 5

The Mirror of Charity . . . . CF 17†

Dialogue on the Soul . . . . CF 22

THE WORKS OF GILBERT OF HOYLAND

Sermons on the Song of Songs I–III . . . . CF 14, 20, 26

Treatises, Sermons, and Epistles . . CF 34

OTHER EARLY CISTERCIAN WRITERS

The Letters of Adam of Perseigne, I . CF 21

Alan of Lille: The Art of Preaching . CF 23

John of Ford. Sermons on the Final Verses of the Song of Songs, I–IV . . . . CF 29, 39, 43, 44

Idung of Prüfening. Cistercians and Cluniacs: The Case for Cîteaux . . CF 33

The Way of Love . . . . CF 16

Guerric of Igny. Liturgical Sermons I–II . . . . CF 8, 32

Three Treatises on Man: A Cistercian Anthropology . . . . CF 24

Isaac of Stella. Sermons on the Christian Year, I . . . . CF 11

Stephen of Lexington. Letters from Ireland . . . . CF 28

THE CISTERCIAN STUDIES SERIES

MONASTIC TEXTS

Evagrius Ponticus. Praktikos and Chapters on Prayer . . . . CS 4

The Rule of the Master . . . . CS 6

The Lives of the Desert Fathers . . . CS 34

Dorotheos of Gaza. Discourses and Sayings . . . . CS 33

Pachomian Koinona I–III:
The Lives . . . . CS 45
The Chronicles and Rules . . . . . CS 46
The Instructions, Letters and Other Writings of St Pachomius and His Disciples . . . . CS 47

Temporarily out of print   †Forthcoming

Symeon the New Theologian. Theological and Practical Treatises and Three Theological Discourses . . . CS 41

Guigo II the Carthusian. The Ladder of Monks and Twelve Meditations . CS 48

The Monastic Rule of Iosif Volotsky . . . . CS 36

CHRISTIAN SPIRITUALITY

The Spirituality of Western Christendom . . . . CS 30

Russian Mystics (Sergius Bolshakoff) CS 26

In Quest of the Absolute: The Life and Works of Jules Monchanin (J. G. Weber) . . . . CS 51

The Name of Jesus (Irenée Hausherr) . . . . CS 44

Entirely for God: A Life of Cyprian Tansi (Elizabeth Isichei) . . . . CS 43

Abba: Guides to Wholeness and Holiness East and West . . . . CS 38

MONASTIC STUDIES

The Abbot in Monastic Tradition (Pierre Salmon) . . . . CS 14

Why Monks? (François Vandenbroucke) . . . . CS 17

Silence in the Rule of St Benedict (Ambrose Wathen) . . . . CS 22

One Yet Two: Monastic Tradition East and West . . . . CS 29

Community and Abbot in the Rule of St Benedict I (Adalbert de Vogüé) . CS 5/1

Consider Your Call: A Theology of the Monastic Life (Daniel Rees et al) . CS 20

Households of God (David Parry) . . CS 39

CISTERCIAN STUDIES

The Cistercian Spirit (M. Basil Pennington, ed.) . . . . . . CS 3

The Eleventh-Century Background of Cîteaux (Bede K. Lackner) . . . . . . CS 8

Contemplative Community . . . . CS 21

Cistercian Sign Language (Robert Barakat) . . . . CS 11

The Cistercians in Denmark (Brian P. McGuire) . . . . CS 35

Saint Bernard of Clairvaux: Essays Commemorating the Eighth Centenary of His Canonization . . CS 28

Bernard of Clairvaux: Studies Presented to Dom Jean Leclercq . . . . CS 23

Bernard of Clairvaux and the Cistercian Spirit (Jean Leclercq) . . . . CS 16

William of St Thierry: The Man and His Work (J. M. Déchanet) . . . . CS 10

Aelred of Rievaulx: A Study (Aelred Squire) . . . . CS 50

Christ the Way: The Christology of Guerric of Igny (John Morson) . . CS 25

The Golden Chain: The Theological Anthropology of Isaac of Stella (Bernard McGinn) . . . . CS 15

Studies in Cistercian Art and Architecture, I (Meredith Lillich, ed) . . CS 66

Studies in Medieval Cistercian History sub-series

Studies I . . . . CS 13

Studies II . . . . CS 24

Cistercian Ideals and Reality (Studies III) . . . . CS 60

Simplicity and Ordinariness (Studies IV) . . . . CS 61

The Chimera of His Age: Studies on St Bernard (Studies V) . . . . CS 63

Cistercians in the Late Middle Ages (Studies VI) . . . . CS 64

Noble Piety and Reformed Monasticism (Studies VII) . . . . CS 65

Benedictus: Studies in Honor of St Benedict of Nursia (Studies VIII) . CS 67

Heaven on Earth (Studies IX) . . . . CS 68†

THOMAS MERTON

The Climate of Monastic Prayer . . . . CS 1

Thomas Merton on St Bernard . . . . . CS 9

Thomas Merton's Shared Contemplation: A Protestant Perspective (Daniel J. Adams) . . . . CS 62

Solitude in the Writings of Thomas Merton (Richard Anthony Cashen) . . . . . CS 40

The Message of Thomas Merton (Brother Patrick Hart, ed.) . . . . . CS 42

FAIRACRES PRESS, OXFORD

The Wisdom of the Desert Fathers

The Letters of St Antony the Great

The Letters of Ammonas, Successor of St Antony

A Study of Wisdom. Three Tracts by the author of *The Cloud of Unknowing*

The Power of the Name. The Jesus Prayer in Orthodox Spirituality (Kallistos Ware)

Solitude and Communion

Contemporary Monasticism

A Pilgrim's Book of Prayers (Gilbert Shaw)

Theology and Spirituality (Andrew Louth)

Temporarily out of print   †*Forthcoming*